Christian Living

The Spirituality of the
Foyers of Charity

By the same author

Understanding Medjugorje: Heavenly Visions or Religious Illusion? (Theotokos, Nottingham, 2006)

Marian Apparitions, the Bible, and the Modern World, (Gracewing, Leominster, 2002)

Italian translation:

Il libro delle Apparizioni Mariane, (Gribaudi, Milan, 2004)

Apparitions of Mary: Their Meaning in History, (Catholic Truth Society, London, 2000)

More details at: www.theotokos.org.uk

Further copies of this book can be ordered online securely using a credit card at:

www.theotokos.org.uk/pages/books/books.html

or you can order copies via online booksellers, or through your local bookseller.

Christian Living

The Spirituality of the Foyers of Charity

Donal Anthony Foley

Based on Conferences given by Fr Michel Tierny

Theotokos Books

Published by Theotokos Books
PO Box 8570, Nottingham, England

www.theotokos.org.uk
books@theotokos.org.uk

First Published in 2006

Cover photograph of the Foyer of Charity at Courset,
France, courtesy of the Foyer Community

Cover design/implemenation by Mike Daley

ISBN 0955074614

Contents

Acknowledgements

I would like to thank the following for their help in the preparation and production of this book. Father Michel Tierny, the Father of the Foyer of Charity at Courset, in France, for permission to use his retreat material, as well as those members of the community who read the text. Thanks also particularly to Martin Blake for reading the text, and for his helpful advice and comments, and to Leo Madigan, and Dr Pravin Thevathasan for similar assistance. Thanks, too, to Rev. Paul Dean and to Fr David Hartley for their help, and finally, I am very grateful to Fr Ian Ker for kindly providing a foreword.

Foreword by Fr Ian Ker

Pope John Paul II called the rediscovery of the charismatic dimension of the Church one of the most significant achievements of the Second Vatican Council. At certain times in history, the Holy Spirit has inspired charismatic movements of the greatest importance for the Church. The most outstanding examples are the rise of monasticism in the third century, of the mendicant friars of the thirteenth century, of the Jesuits in the sixteenth century, and all the other active orders and congregations that followed, particularly of women missionaries, in the nineteenth century. The Pope clearly saw the rise of the ecclesial movements and communities in the twentieth century as another great charismatic surge with the same potential both for evangelization and for the renewal of the Church.

Hans Urs von Balthasar has pointed out that in the history of the Church charisms come "like a bolt of lightning from the blue, destined to illuminate a single and original point of God's will for the Church in a given time." Given that the ecclesial communities and movements do in fact realize concretely the fundamental ecclesiology of Vatican II, they would indeed seem very pertinently to illustrate Balthasar's point. The first two seminal chapters of *Lumen Gentium*, the constitution on the Church, describe the Church in scriptural and patristic terms as being essentially an organic communion of the baptized faithful upon whom the Holy Spirit bestows both hierarchical and charismatic gifts. This is not a Church with the clergy on the one side and the laity on the other, but a Church consisting of Christians with many different and varying gifts and roles, albeit one that is a hierarchical Church, in which the ultimate authentication and discernment of the genuine fruits of the Spirit is entrusted to the successors of Peter and the other Apostles.

In 1999, the Holy See approved the statues of the Foyers of Charity, which were founded in France in 1936 by a remarkable woman called Marthe Robin, whose cause for beatification is well advanced, in collaboration with her spiritual director, Fr Georges Finet. The Foyers, which anticipated the teaching of the Council on the Church as an organic community, consist of a Priest, who is the Father, living in community with consecrated lay men and women who are not canonically religious but who do embrace the evangelical precepts of chastity, poverty, and obedience. In some Foyers there are also families sharing in the community life. And beyond the confines of the Foyers is an extended family of Christians who support the Foyers through whose retreats and spirituality their own lives have been changed and enriched.

This slim book, attractively and simply written, gives us the authentic flavour of a Foyer retreat. It will be of interest to those who, like John Paul II, see the ecclesial communities and movements as God's answer to the dream of John XXIII, the pope responsible for calling the Second Vatican Council, for a new Pentecost. It will be compulsive reading for anyone fascinated by Marthe Robin, whose spiritual influence on the Church in France can still be felt today, as well as for anyone interested in attending a retreat in one of the Foyers—or even contemplating joining one. And finally, it is ideal spiritual reading for the general reader. Perhaps it may even inspire the founding of a Foyer of Charity in one of the British Isles, where the Church is in such need of renewal.

Introduction

This book came about because I attended a series of retreats, during the 1990s, at the Foyer of Charity at Courset near Boulogne in France. A group of English speaking retreatants were welcomed at the Foyer for a number of years and the retreat conferences were simultaneously translated into English. These retreats were given by Fr Michel Tierny and during them I made extensive notes, with the idea in the back of my mind that one day they might make interesting and inspirational reading—this book is the result.

Fr Tierny established the Foyer at Courset in the early 1970s to serve the northeast corner of France. It comprises a beautiful nineteenth-century château surrounded by a park, but there has been much new building, including additional accommodation for retreatants and a recently completed chapel. Before becoming the Father of the Courset Foyer, Fr Tierny was a professor at the Seminary in Lille. The community has now grown much larger, and, apart from retreat work, Courset also has a school with 200 pupils— indeed a good many members of the Foyer are teachers.

I have tried to preserve Fr Tierny's style and give the reader some idea of what it is like to actually attend a Foyer retreat, but rather than reproduce his retreat conferences in the exact order in which they were given, I have rearranged the material thematically, so that particular topics are dealt with in successive sections of the book. There is some repetition of important points, but I feel this is useful by way of emphasis. Despite these changes, this book does follow the general pattern of many Foyer retreats, in that it begins with idea of discipleship, our call as Christians, before moving on through topics such as prayer, the Trinity, the sacraments, and so on. And just as in a Foyer retreat, the climax of the book is the Passion and Resurrection of Christ, and the consecration to Mary following the method of St Louis de Montfort.

I feel that this book is suitable not only for those who want to know more about the spirituality of Marthe Robin and the Foyers of Charity, but also for those who are looking for general spiritual reading. Similarly, it might be helpful for those wanting to conduct their own "do-it-yourself" retreat. The important point is that this book is meant to be read slowly and meditatively, and that readers should almost try and put themselves in the position of people hearing the Gospel for the first time—and this is indeed one of the aims of a Foyer retreat, to help us to look at Christian teaching in a new light.

The first chapter outlines the life and spirituality of Marthe Robin—including the founding of the Foyers of Charity—as well as Marthe's vision for the Foyers, and it also has some information about the positive attitude of the Church towards both the Foyers and Marthe. Subsequent chapters are, as explained above, a thematic arrangement of some of Fr Tierny's retreat conferences on the basic principles of the Christian life.

1

Marthe Robin & the Foyers of Charity

On 10 February 1936, a young Priest in his thirties named Georges Finet drove from the city of Lyon, in south-eastern France, to the village of Châteauneuf-de-Galaure in the Drôme foothills, to visit Marthe Robin. He carried in his car a hand-colored picture of Mary Mediatrix of All Graces, which a mutual friend had asked him to deliver personally to her.

Marthe lived with her parents in a small farmhouse a mile from the village. Born in 1902, the youngest of five children, she had been bedridden since 1928, and from 1929 more of less paralyzed. Already she had a reputation for living in the closest possible mystical union with Christ and His Mother, and in October 1930 she had been marked with the stigmata of His Passion; every Friday she relived His sufferings on the Cross.

This meeting was to prove providential, for it led to a collaboration between Marthe and Père Finet which would only be broken by her death in 1981, by which time there would be some sixty Foyers of Charity in five continents. Since then, even more communities have been founded.

In the course of three hours of conversation, Marthe convinced the Abbé Finet that his vocation lay in helping her. For the first hour they spoke of the Blessed Virgin and her role in the Church. Fr Finet, who gave Marian conferences on the teaching of St Louis de Montfort, was astonished at the depth of her insights. At three o'clock she began to talk of the great events which were soon to occur in the world, some very painful, presumably a reference to World War II and its aftermath, others rich in graces, usually taken as a reference to the Second Vatican Council. She announced "a New Pentecost of Love," and a renewal of the Church by means of the laity. This would take many forms, but outstanding in this process would be the Foyers, "Hearths" of Light, Charity and Love.

These were to be made up of consecrated lay persons and directed by a Priest, the Father of the Foyer; their main task would be to provide week-long silent retreats to be given by him. Marthe maintained that the Foyers would have a worldwide influence, and would particularly be "an expression of the Heart of Jesus to the nations after the defeat of materialism and satanic errors." Amongst these she mentioned communism, and Freemasonry.

After this, Marthe asked the Abbé Finet to come to Châteauneuf to found the first Foyer of Charity, telling him that this was the express wish of God. She also told him that, amongst other things, he would preach retreats, initially for women and girls, and that these would have to be held in silence, with the first one to take place the following September. She reassured him as to publicity about these and the necessary finance, telling him that the Blessed Virgin would take care of everything. He said he was willing but would have to ask permission from his superiors. Abbé Finet's superior, Msgr. Bornet agreed to let him go. So did the Vicar-general of Lyon. Finally his spiritual director, a professor of theology at the university, was enthusiastic about the idea— he had already met Marthe. Thus seven months later the first retreat was conducted for thirty-three persons, all women, several of whom would become permanent members of the original Foyer at Châteauneuf. (Fr Raymond Peyret, *Marthe Robin: The Cross and the Joy*, Alba House, New York, 1983, pp. 75-78).

Marthe's influence and spirituality

Marthe Robin would appear to be for the second half of the twentieth century, and beyond, what St Thérèse of Lisieux was for the first half. And indeed the two women are closely linked spiritually, despite the fact that whereas Thérèse died aged twenty-four and became known through her autobiography, and thus famous throughout the Catholic world, Marthe lived to be seventy-nine, and the greater part of her life was spent in seclusion, entirely immobilized in a small room at her parents' house.

Mystically united to Christ and His Mother, she was visited by most of the retreatants who came to Châteauneuf over a period of fifty years. It has been estimated that she may have met one hundred thousand people; each one waited in the little kitchen and was allowed ten minutes with Marthe in her darkened room. She showed a keen interest in the affairs of each visitor, gave sound advice, and always finished by praying with him or her.

She had extraordinary insights into the concerns of those who sought her counsel, and many testified to how much a visit to Marthe had meant to them, in solving a family problem, or obtaining light as to what direction they should take in life. A number of other growing communities originating in France, including the Community of Saint John, owe their foundations partly to her support. Although she was paralyzed and could not actually write herself, she dictated a large collection of prayers, meditations and observations, which are gradually being published, and a large number of books, mostly still in French, have been written about her. She is constantly quoted in the Foyers.

Perhaps her most striking spiritual document was her "Act of Consecration," made in 1925 at the age of twenty-three. In this masterpiece of spiritual thought the word "love" appears twenty-two times, but "justice" not once. From then on she was consecrated through Mary to Jesus to be a living sacrifice to God. She never attended a public Mass after 1928, yet her whole life was like a Mass, a perfect oblation of thanksgiving, united to the sacrifice of Christ on the Cross, and inspired by love. As she herself put it, in February 1930: "One can only make people love to the extent that one possesses it, just as one can only radiate light if one carries within oneself the truth which is light."

Marthe Robin and the Foyer Retreats

Foyer retreats are silent and generally last five days. They usually comprise three or four conferences each day, at which the Priest expounds various Christian themes, depending on the particular retreat. Mass is also celebrated daily and there is time for adoration, the Rosary and private prayer. Meals are taken in silence but accompanied by classical music. The main idea is that a peaceful and prayerful atmosphere will enable the teachings to sink in and to deeply influence the retreatant—that is why silence is so important.

Marthe's prayer was that those on retreat, and indeed all believers, should be able to fix their minds and hearts on God with respectful attention, that they should correspond with grace and have a continuous disposition for, and awareness of, the Holy Trinity. Marthe wanted all sorts of people to come on the retreats—believers, unbelievers, everyone; she wanted them to experience that the Word of God is meant for all. The silence of the Foyer retreat helps people to discover God's tenderness; to hear God in their hearts. Marthe felt that the retreats were great moments of grace and opportunities for catechetical teaching, as well as a form of training for contemplation. She saw them as helping people to assimilate Christian doctrine by careful study and meditation, to take it into their hearts and really understand it, before passing it on to others.

Foyer retreats are about God as Father teaching His children to live a Christian life; He corrects them and puts them on the right road. Jesus gives them the joy to live in the love of the Father. This was the intuition of Marthe; that God carries and supports those who trust in Him. Marthe didn't just want formal catechetics, she also wanted something which would touch people's hearts. There is some repetition during a retreat because it often takes a while for ideas to sink in. Most people, though, should be able to cope with the discipline of a retreat; they receive spiritual help from the prayers and the self-offering of the members of the Foyer.

Marthe wanted the retreatants to be welcomed with love, and for the food to be fresh and well cooked; but she did demand silence and was insistent on that; it is part of the sacrificial attitude required for the retreat, because this is the way we hear what God is saying to us. Marthe understood that austerity isn't absolutely necessary, that it can cause people to give up. But she insisted, too, that without silence they wouldn't realise their vocation, or only realise it superficially. They might do good things but not necessarily what God wants. So there is a requirement to go within, a requirement for recollection, and this is impossible without silence. This also requires a generous and constant sacrifice.

Marthe contended that all those on retreat have a direct relationship with Mary, since she is the mother of the Foyer. Mary offers her spiritual children to God. Retreatants were called not to fix their ideas exclusively on exterior things: rather, like Mary, they were to aim at interior meditation. Mary would help them, and so the aim was to try to discover one's real aims and aspirations during a retreat, to become aware of the importance of trying harder after being on retreat.

For Marthe, Mary was a mother who was discrete and yet eminently present to her children, and she insisted on the need to be thankful to Mary for introducing retreatants to the spirituality of the Foyers of Charity, which is nothing less than the spirituality of genuine Christian living.

Clearly, the above observations also apply to those who read a book such as this one, which contains the essentials of the spirituality of the Foyers.

The Church and the Foyers of Charity

We can get some idea of how Pope Paul VI understood Marthe's vocation, and that of the Foyers, by considering these words of his: "The Foyers give an authentic doctrinal and spiritual teaching in a climate of silence, charity, and devotion to Mary, which opens souls to conversion, deepens their life with God and leads them to the apostolate."

This papal approval has been reflected in the general attitude of the Church towards Marthe. The Bishop of Valence established a Commission of Enquiry regarding her in February 1988, and in March 1991 the Holy See gave its "nihil obstat" to the official opening of a Diocesan Cause; the Commission completed its work in 1996 and submitted a text of 17,000 pages to Rome. Since then it has been in the hands of the Congregation for the Causes of the Saints. Thus Marthe's Cause is advancing in Rome. In a letter to Père Michon, who currently heads the Foyer movement worldwide, dated 26 February 2002, Mgsr Rylko, the Secretary of the Pontifical Congregation for the Laity, wrote approvingly of both Marthe and the Foyers.

But even before the above developments, the Pontifical Council for the Laity had, in 1986, issued the following statement about the Foyers, fifty years after the foundation of the first community:

> The purpose of the Work of the Foyers of Charity, which started in France in 1936 at the initiative of Marthe Robin and her spiritual director Fr Finet, is to form lay people in appropriate centers—the Foyers—thus preparing them to contribute to the renewal of the Church in view of the evangelization of the world. This formation is principally given through the retreats where the participants receive the teaching of the Word of God and celebrate the Eucharist, while also taking part in adoration,

and Marian prayer. The Foyers of Charity welcome all those who come, believers and unbelievers alike, to seek the light of Christ and to receive the teaching of the Church. They do this without distinction of nationality, race, or social situation. Foyers of Charity can also have other branches of activity and apostolate according to the needs of the local Churches and the talents of the members.

Although each Foyer is found in a diocese and is integrated into the life of a local Church, all the Foyers of Charity form a single, large, spiritual family, living the same mission according to the same Spirit. The tangible sign and the guarantee of this unity are the manifest attachment of each Foyer to the Foyer Centre of Châteauneuf de Galaure, in which the original grace took shape, and which remains the visible symbol of the charism of the Work.

In celebrating the fiftieth anniversary of its foundation, the Work of the Foyers of Charity, rich in graces received throughout its history, and desirous of rooting itself more deeply in the Church in order to accomplish its mission for the world, asked the Pontifical Council of the Laity to recognize it officially and to approve its statutes.

After careful study of the documentation presented by those responsible for the Work of the Foyers of Charity, with a positive evaluation from many bishops with a Foyer in their diocese, and after submitting the request for recognition to His Holiness Pope John Paul II, the Pontifical Council for the laity recognizes the Work of the "Foyers of Charity" as a private association of the faithful of international character according to the norms established by canons 321-326, and approves their canonical structure ad experimentimum for a period of three years.

Eduardo Card. Pironio, President Paul J. Cordes, Vice-President; Given at the Vatican, on the Solemnity of All Saints, November 1, 1986

As is common, this period was extended, and since then, on December 8th 1999, Cardinal Stafford approved the Canonical Structures of the Foyers of Charity, for the

Pontifical Council for the Laity, as the following document indicates:

> Taking in consideration the request of the Father in Charge of the Work of the Foyers de Charité to the Pontifical Council for the Laity, by letter, on the 15th August 1999, in view of the permanent approval of the Statutes of the Work of the 'Foyers de Charité'; In view of the numerous letters supporting this request from Ordinaries of the dioceses where 'Foyers de Charité' have been established, giving witness to the quality of their evangelical life, their firm rooting in the Church and the spiritual radiation of their service; Taking into account that, in recent years, new 'Foyers de Charité' have been opened, and often at the invitation of the Bishops themselves, and that the life of the 'Foyers de Charité' on the different continents has been enriched with new vocations;
>
> Finally, having appreciated the effort of deep reflection which has been made by the 'Foyers de Charité' these last few years concerning the charisma of their origins, as well as several key questions indicated by the Dicaster, The Pontifical Council for the Laity confirms the recognition of the Work of the Foyers de Charité as an international private Association of the faithful of Pontifical law, endowed with a juridical personality, according to Canon norms 298-311 and 321-329 of CIC and the permanent approval of its Statutes, whose original text has been authenticated and placed in the archives of this Dicaster.
>
> Given at the Vatican, on the 8th December 1999 at the Solemnity of the Immaculate Conception.

2

Discipleship: Our Call
to Follow Christ

God "desires all men to be saved and to come to the knowledge of the truth": that is, of Christ Jesus. Christ must be proclaimed to all nations and individuals, so that this revelation may reach to the ends of the earth: God graciously arranged that the things he had once revealed for the salvation of all peoples should remain in their entirety, throughout the ages, and be transmitted to all generations. (*Catechism of the Catholic Church*, 74)

We are the Apostles of the new evangelization. We must meditate on the fact that we are sent by God. It is, however, difficult to keep our vocation—the attractions of the world tend to distract us. When we are sent into the world, Christ speaks through us, and we are united more closely to Him than our soul is to our body. Jesus speaks by and through us, the baptised people who are the light of nations—*Lumen Gentium*. We are both the body of Christ and the thought of Christ when we act in this way. The Father gives us His revelation through the Son and we then have the task of passing it on. Our religion is a revelation and not a natural religion.

Our mission is to bring the people we live amongst towards Christ. It is not enough just to talk to them, more interiority is needed, something which comes from true contact with Jesus. His injunction to "take and eat" is a reality, but we mustn't get indigestion from "eating" too quickly, and also we shouldn't just eat alone—we must pray with others. We are also called to be "prophets," that is people who speak out. The fact that we are ordinary people doesn't matter; it is the manner of our action which is important. But we can also witness to Christ without actually saying anything, as did St Francis of Assisi who said: "Everywhere I go I preach the Gospel—sometimes I use words."

The Witness of John the Baptist

And this is the testimony of John, when the Jews sent priests and Levites from Jerusalem to ask him, "Who are you?" He confessed, he did not deny, but confessed, "I am not the Christ." And they asked him, "What then? Are you Elijah?" He said, "I am not." "Are you the prophet?" And he answered, "No." They said to him then, "Who are you? Let us have an answer for those who sent us. What do you say about yourself?" He said, "I am the voice of one crying in the wilderness, 'Make straight the way of the Lord,' as the prophet Isaiah said."

Now they had been sent from the Pharisees. They asked him, "Then why are you baptizing, if you are neither the Christ, nor Elijah, nor the prophet?" John answered them, "I baptize with water; but among you stands one whom you do not know, even he who comes after me, the thong of whose sandal I am not worthy to untie." This took place in Bethany beyond the Jordan, where John was baptizing. (John 1:19-28)

Jesus was presented by John the Baptist in an extraordinary way. John is the only saint, apart from Our Lady, to have his birth celebrated; usually the feast day commemorates the death of a saint—their entrance into heaven. He was educated in the womb of Elizabeth, who recognised the Mother of God when her child moved within her own womb.

It's difficult to classify John; he had a desire for purification in the Old Testament tradition of Isaiah, who saw himself as impure before God, but was cleansed from his sin. John wanted to purify himself for his role as precursor of Jesus, the friend of the bridegroom. He went into solitude to live a difficult, dangerous and painful life: he wasn't going to improve his education, nor to gain earthly things. The Jewish authorities wanted to question John; he told them he wasn't the Messiah or Elijah or the Prophet. He said he was a voice crying in the desert, announcing Christ, whose sandal straps he was unfit to undo.

> The next day he saw Jesus coming toward him, and said, "Behold, the Lamb of God, who takes away the sin of the world! This is he of whom I said, 'After me comes a man who ranks before me, for he was before me.' I myself did not know him; but for this I came baptizing with water, that he might be revealed to Israel." And John bore witness, "I saw the Spirit descend as a dove from heaven, and it remained on him. I myself did not know him; but he who sent me to baptize with water said to me, 'He on whom you see the Spirit descend and remain, this is he who baptizes with the Holy Spirit.' And I have seen and have borne witness that this is the Son of God." (John 1:29-34)

John saw Jesus as the Lamb of God—he understood Jesus at a deeper level when the Spirit came down and rested on Our Lord. He was a witness that Jesus was the Son of God and was full of joy to discover Him.

The First Disciples

We need to slowly read and meditate on the following Scripture passage about the calling of the first disciples from John's Gospel, going carefully over each word. St John the evangelist, who wrote his Gospel after meditating on the events he had seen during the whole course of his life, was a true contemplative.

The next day again John was standing with two of his disciples; and he looked at Jesus as he walked, and said, "Behold, the Lamb of God!" The two disciples heard him say this, and they followed Jesus. Jesus turned, and saw them following, and said to them, "What do you seek?" And they said to him, "Rabbi" (which means Teacher), "where are you staying?" He said to them, "Come and see." They came and saw where he was staying; and they stayed with him that day, for it was about the tenth hour. (John 1:35-39).

John the Baptist's two disciples, Andrew and John, were present when he looked intently at Jesus, a look of contemplation, in describing Him as the "Lamb of God." Jesus was the Passover Lamb, taking the people out of their slavery through the desert to the Promised Land. John and Andrew followed Jesus, staying with Him that evening. They asked Jesus where He lived, which was asking at a deeper level what His intuitions were, what His interior nourishment was; they wanted to find out more about Him. Jesus said "Come and see"—He wanted them to experience His love. The will is superior to the intellect and goes towards its goal; they stayed with Him.

One of the two who heard John speak, and followed him, was Andrew, Simon Peter's brother. He first found his brother Simon, and said to him, "We have found the Messiah" (which means Christ). He brought him to Jesus. Jesus looked at him, and said, "So you are Simon the son of John? You shall be called Cephas" (which means Peter). The next day Jesus decided to go to Galilee. And he found Philip and said to him, "Follow me." Now Philip was from Bethsaida, the city of Andrew and Peter. Philip found Nathanael, and said to him, "We have found him of whom Moses in the law and also the prophets wrote, Jesus of Nazareth, the son of Joseph." Nathanael said to him, "Can anything good come out of Nazareth?" Philip said to him, "Come and see."

Jesus saw Nathanael coming to him, and said of him, "Behold, an Israelite indeed, in whom is no guile!" Nathanael said to him, "How do you know me?" Jesus answered him, "Before Philip called you, when you were under the fig tree, I saw you." Nathanael answered him, "Rabbi, you are the Son of God! You are the King of Israel!" Jesus answered him, "Because I said to you, I saw you under the fig tree, do you believe? You shall see greater things than these." And he said to him, "Truly, truly, I say to you, you will see heaven opened, and the angels of God ascending and descending upon the Son of man." (John 1:40-51)

So the disciples penetrated and experienced the Heart of Jesus, and decided to transfer their allegiance from John to Jesus. They introduced Peter to Jesus, who gave him his new name, a sign of his new mission as the future head of the Church. Philip was called the next day, as was Nathanael, who had asked if anything good could come from Nazareth. Jesus had Nathanael in His heart and told him about Jacob's ladder.

The Holy Spirit gives us the strength to keep going and we gain further by meditating on Jesus' life. By contemplating Him we become more like Him. God isn't treating us as strangers—no other religion has a God who comes so close to Man.

Discipleship and the Cross

And Jesus went on with his disciples, to the villages of Caesarea Philipi; and on the way he asked his disciples, "Who do men say that I am?" And they told him, "John the Baptist; and others say, Elijah; and others one of the prophets." And he asked them, "But who do you say that I am?" Peter answered him, "You are the Christ." And he charged them to tell no one about him. And he began to teach them that the Son of man must suffer many things, and be rejected by the elders and the chief priests and the scribes, and be killed, and after three days rise again. And he said this plainly. And Peter took him, and began to rebuke him. But turning and seeing his disciples, he rebuked

Peter, and said, "Get behind me, Satan! For you are not on the side of God, but of men." (Mark 8:27-33)

We can't expect to change ourselves quickly—it takes a long time to understand the Cross. Peter saw Jesus as the Messiah and Son of God; Jesus told His disciples not to tell anyone this. The Jews were expecting a conquering Messiah, so Jesus had to slowly change their thinking. Thus when Peter thought he understood, Jesus told him that he didn't really understand at all, that it was necessary that He, Jesus, had to suffer and die. Peter remonstrated with Jesus, but was rebuked for not wishing to learn as Jesus wanted Him to.

The "Messianic" secret is emphasised in Mark's Gospel; the disciples didn't understand this, but didn't question Jesus. We too will have difficulty understanding. Jesus hid His divinity in the Father so as to lead His disciples in a more human sense.

> And they were on the road, going up to Jerusalem, and Jesus was walking ahead of them; and they were amazed, and those who followed were afraid. And taking the twelve again, he began to tell them what was to happen to him, saying, "Behold, we are going up to Jerusalem; and the Son of man will be delivered to the chief priests and the scribes, and they will condemn him to death, and deliver him to the Gentiles; and they will mock him, and spit upon him, and scourge him, and kill him; and after three days he will rise." (Mark 10:32-34)

On the road to Jerusalem, the disciples were afraid. Jesus explained His Passion, from the heart, with clarity. His greatest pain was the request of James and John for honors. So the leading apostles didn't understand Jesus despite His repeated teachings; they were looking for glory. This is the wisdom of the Gospel and it is difficult for us to understand this fully. We need to immerse ourselves in the heart of Mary—how did she love and understand this mystery, the mystery of the Cross? As our Mother she will help us to understand this, to receive all the graces available to those who undergo the way of the Cross.

Our Call to Discipleship

We, too, are prophets called to witness to Jesus, as Jesus was a witness to the Father, sent by Him. The Father told the Son to come into the world and the Spirit fulfilled this work. Jesus said that those who see Him see the Father. Now we wait for Jesus' second coming from the Father. He chose us and in responding to this choice we restore our hearts. Jesus sends us as the Father sent Him. A sending which continues as the Father continues to send the Son and the Spirit into our hearts—this wasn't done once and for all.

The teaching of the Church continues and develops with time to meet changing conditions, but its essence stays the same. We need to keep in touch with the source of all things, the Father: as Jesus said, he who does not build with me scatters. Listen to His "sending" everyday: but listen interiorly with discernment. St Ambrose spoke much of the sending by the Father, through the Son. We must give our hearts to them. He is always calling, a decisive call, which we must accept in trust. We must say "yes" to the sacramental offering of self by Jesus in the Eucharist; there is a similarity here with the way married couples must offer themselves to their spouses.

Jesus said to pray to the Lord of the harvest to send labourers to gather in the harvest. For us this means teachers and Priests: these vocations need help and preparation. It is still possible for vocations to happen in our society; the great Fathers of the Church were formed in the pagan Greco-Roman world. Follow your vocation to the end as long as the Holy Spirit shows there is a task to be done. Our strength, will, and capacity to share need to be infused by the grace of the Holy Spirit, in order to achieve His aims. Remember each of the disciples was sent according to their own gifts. Marthe was very aware of her vocation, her constant commitment under the Holy Spirit.

Jesus also told us in St John's Gospel, during his Last Supper discourse, how we can prove our discipleship is genuine: "By this all men will know that you are my disciples, if you have love for one another," and again: "If you abide in me, and my words abide in you, ask whatever you will, and it shall be done for you. By this my Father is glorified, that you bear much fruit; and so prove to be my disciples." (John 13:35; 15:7-8). Thus our discipleship depends on abiding in God's love and in turn showing this love to those around us.

We have to work in the same way that Jesus did, and as the *Catechism of the Catholic Church* puts it:

> By reason of their special vocation it belongs to the laity to seek the kingdom of God by engaging in temporal affairs and directing them according to God's will.... It pertains to them in a special way so to illuminate and order all temporal things with which they are closely associated that these may always be effected and grow according to Christ and may be to the glory of the Creator and Redeemer. (CCC 898)

Developing our Gifts

All the gifts and aptitudes we have are ultimately for the purpose of gaining eternal life, and so we must discover these and see how they can help others. The parable of the talents refers to this, and it is really concerned with the talents of our heart and person. We have to offer our gifts to the community, our fundamental gifts, and this goes much deeper than skills like teaching. We need to use our gifts. These deeper gifts are given to us so that others will grow in faith. We must ask what we do for young people and how we can help them to discover their gifts and grow in faith. Everyone needs this help and regrettably some parents are too discreet in this; this is an area where the godparents can be a great help—Marthe's vocation came from her godparents.

Much love is needed to develop the gifts of others; they can be smothered by negative experiences. God's call, our vocation, is generally mediated through others, in the sense of people helping us by making suggestions, and to realize that God loves us. We can help to form the vocation of others, and must realize that we ourselves are not chosen for a particular role because of our merits: all is due to God's choice. The Spirit distributes His gifts as He chooses—but they need to be fostered by us. God doesn't look at the exterior but at the heart. The very depths of our hearts are reserved to God. Christ builds up His body, the Church, in its totality; prayer helps us to understand this:

> The vocation of humanity is to show forth the image of God and to be transformed into the image of the Father's only Son. This vocation takes a personal form since each of us is called to enter into the divine beatitude; it also concerns the human community as a whole. (CCC 1877)

3

Holiness: Our Call to Perfection

"All Christians in any state or walk of life are called to the fullness of Christian life and to the perfection of charity." All are called to holiness: "Be perfect, as your heavenly Father is perfect" ... The way of perfection passes by way of the Cross. There is no holiness without renunciation and spiritual battle. Spiritual progress entails the ascesis and mortification that gradually lead to living in the peace and joy of the Beatitudes. (CCC 2013, 2015)

Jesus' life at Nazareth is important both for the Foyers and the Church. It implies for us an ordinary life but one which involves close union with God. Common sanctity means that we are all called to holiness. We must "feed" our souls with religious practices and have a desire for perfection before God.

It is necessary for us to become like God—this means being obedient and crucified. The "simplicity" of holiness is for all. Holiness is not the same as the graces of healing, prophecy, visions, and so on, as found in the lives of the saints. Holiness involves being simple, pure and harmonious, and is possible even in the most ordinary life, as long as we aim for a closer union with God. All are called to discover the message of Jesus, and for this we need a spiritual hunger. "Ordinary" people tend to see holiness as too difficult for them; but each person can reach "ordinary" holiness without miracles, or exceptional events, as, for example, in the hidden life of St Thérèse of Lisieux. She became a saint through a simple life, but one full of love: what is certain is that we won't get straight to heaven by being mediocre. The life of the Holy Family in Nazareth was very ordinary. Even though Jesus was God, the second person of the Trinity, whose actions are divine and thus to be adored, He lived a very simple, humble, hidden life for thirty years. We need to meditate on why He chose this sort of life. This secret, silent, life with Mary and Joseph was a life of love. This is also the sort of life that is lived in the Foyers, one of prayer, work, meals, an ordinary life. We must put an effort into our lives to reproduce the life lived in Nazareth.

We are required to sanctify ourselves in order to become true "missionaries." The important thing is the intention with which we do things—remove whatever is not worthy of a Christian. In the Incarnation, Christ veiled the glory of His divinity and became like us. Christ is at the heart of the Trinity and we are members of Christ; He is sitting at the right hand of the Father; this is the logic of the Incarnation:

> The unique and altogether singular event of the Incarnation of the Son of God does not mean that Jesus Christ is part God and part man, nor does it imply that he is the result of a confused mixture of the divine and the human. He became truly man while remaining truly God. Jesus Christ is true God and true man. (CCC 464)

Why does He give us His tenderness when He knows we won't appreciate it? The tenderness and mercy of God are infinite; we see this in the Mass where the Lamb of God takes away the sins of the world. We are all repentant sinners and should pray that God will have pity on us.

The Samaritan Woman

> Now when the Lord knew that the Pharisees had heard that Jesus was making and baptizing more disciples than John (although Jesus himself did not baptize, but only his disciples),

> he left Judea and departed again to Galilee. He had to pass through Samaria. So he came to a city of Samaria, called Sychar, near the field that Jacob gave to his son Joseph. Jacob's well was there, and so Jesus, wearied as he was with his journey, sat down beside the well. It was about the sixth hour. (John 4:1-6)

How does this story speak of sanctification to us? Our greatest treasure is our spiritual life; we have to try and avoid sin. But we set so little store by this spiritual life, not taking it seriously enough or putting enough effort into it. This happens because we don't aim high enough.

> There came a woman of Samaria to draw water. Jesus said to her, "Give me a drink." For his disciples had gone away into the city to buy food. The Samaritan woman said to him, "How is it that you, a Jew, ask a drink of me, a woman of Samaria?" For Jews have no dealings with Samaritans. Jesus answered her, "If you knew the gift of God, and who it is that is saying to you, 'Give me a drink,' you would have asked him, and he would have given you living water." The woman said to him, "Sir, you have nothing to draw with, and the well is deep; where do you get that living water? Are you greater than our father Jacob, who gave us the well, and drank from it himself, and his sons, and his cattle?" (John 4:7-12)

Jesus had reached the well and sat down because He was tired: He asked for a drink. The Samaritan woman was suspicious and surprised. Jesus deepened the dialogue with her—if only she knew what God was offering. We don't realise how great is the gift which God is offering us, that is, eternal life. Nor do we realise the greatness of Jesus, the second person of the Trinity made man, God in person. He is saying He is the source of life and we too can have life in abundance. Jesus was talking about living water; the Word made flesh is life itself. God is the true reality, but we limit reality to what we can see: we need to be open to all levels of reality, including the angels and saints, and, of course, God.

We have a great desire for love: we must realise that only God can fulfil this. This means the real life of the Trinity, the indwelling of the Blessed Trinity. Life is transmitted to us by Christ our head, just as sin was transmitted originally to us through Adam's fault. Christ, the new Adam, transcends this—He is the head of the whole of humanity, the head of the mystical body, with His divinity and humanity in the person of the Word.

Just having the divine life in us tends to make us contemplatives. If we have an open heart we receive the divine life from Jesus; this is something that can only be experienced personally and is the path to true contemplation. We need to pursue this type of contemplation all the time and develop a continuous awareness of God's presence. This means living on the interior level where God is.

> Jesus said to her, "Every one who drinks of this water will thirst again, but whoever drinks of the water that I shall give him will never thirst; the water that I shall give him will become in him a spring of water welling up to eternal life." The woman said to him, "Sir, give me this water, that I may not thirst, nor come here to draw." (John 4:13-15)

At this point, the woman didn't recognise Jesus as the Messiah; she was still doubting and lacking in confidence. Ordinary water doesn't give true life—we still remain thirsty. The living water promised by Jesus satisfies our eternal thirst. We need to be open and receptive to this new life. We can recognise this other life; it shows through from time to time in, for example, the beauty of a child's innocence. This idea of "living water" involves and implies a continuous and vital contact between the believer and Jesus. So this eternal life in us is a wonder which turns us to God and takes others with us too. We need, though, to have the right disposition to receive this living water.

The spiritual life isn't just automatic—we have to correspond, to desire it. We have to be purified to really appreciate it. Jesus led the woman to see the truth. Faith tells us about the things we will possess in eternity—but it also allows us to love our brothers and sisters in a much better way than we might think.

Jesus was telling the woman that she had to decide how to live. The divine life in us should involve our being converted, and often, indeed, our failures in life can actually lead to our conversion. We discover the depth of sin, our wounds, and the greatness of eternal life. We realise that we must give our hearts to God.

> Jesus said to her, "Go, call your husband, and come here." The woman answered him, "I have no husband." Jesus said to her, "You are right in saying, 'I have no husband'; for you have had five husbands, and he whom you now have is not your husband; this you said truly." The woman said to him, "Sir, I perceive that you are a prophet. Our fathers worshiped on this mountain; and you say that in Jerusalem is the place where men ought to worship."
>
> Jesus said to her, "Woman, believe me, the hour is coming when neither on this mountain nor in Jerusalem will you worship the Father. You worship what you do not know; we worship what we know, for salvation is from the Jews. But the hour is coming, and now is, when the true worshipers will worship the Father in spirit and truth, for such the Father seeks to worship him. God is spirit, and those who worship him must worship in spirit and truth." The woman said to him, "I know that Messiah is coming (he who is called Christ); when he comes, he will show us all things." Jesus said to her, "I who speak to you am he." (John 4:16-26)

Our Call to Holiness

We should note the words here which imply adoration, that is, a movement of the soul. We are meant to worship God in spirit and in truth, not in sentimentality—this is the sort of worshipper which the Father wants. It is really an attitude of heart, like that of Martha and Mary. We must ask pardon, but must also expiate our sins. Jesus acts like an elder brother amongst us; the Father invites us to grow towards Him—but it isn't magic— work is involved on our part. We have to merit the salvation Jesus has won for us. The one who, like Marthe, suffers, offers and prays is terribly human. Marthe was a victim of love, someone who was given a tremendous mission.

We aren't fully human unless we make efforts to expiate our sins. We have to "earn" our salvation by working for it— otherwise it's not a salvation worthy of man. Jesus worked for our salvation, to encourage us to imitate His love. He loved His own in the world right to the end with great respect and wants us to be drawn to Him through love. He wants us to be transformed by love. He went to the limits of love for His own—death on the Cross.

We have to be aware of our responsibilities in the world; many insults are given to God through war, poverty, and other evils, and we mustn't wash our hands of all this. We pretend it isn't any of our business, and can even contribute to these evils and so are responsible and sinful. We have to reflect on all this and so be able to discover our vocation, which is deeper than just whether to get married or not: it involves God's inner plan for us all. We have been given the grace to understand the mysteries of God, but we must be open to this gift.

Our Responsibility in the Church

We just can't look at the Church with human eyes; the early history of the Church is only understandable through the mystery of the Cross. One holy person, a soul of goodness, can save many others: Christians aren't aware enough of this. We have the honour of carrying out God's work and this means identifying ourselves with Christ. This involves all the ordinary things of life; through our Baptism we can offer up everything. So through Baptism we have responsibility for the salvation of our brothers. We have come from God and we are called to return to God with our hearts full. We must pray for the grace to understand the Heart of Jesus.

The summit of joy for Jesus was the Cross, and we too have to go through this experience of the Cross in an interior sense. This means coping with what is possible for us and not looking for extraordinary burdens. We will see our vocation afterwards; Paul was accused of being mad and even Peter couldn't accept the shame of the Cross. Don't commit yourself to a particular direction without this inner life and understanding, so that you are really in contact with God.

Jesus started His life for God, His mission, at the time of His Baptism. God gives us His gifts in due proportion. Have we really understood how much Jesus loved us? Most of us reply to this love quite badly. Our wisdom doesn't always correspond to our age—true wisdom comes from God. We are all consecrated by Baptism and have a vocation. Our responsibility is to the whole world, to redeem our brothers. It means accepting things which go against us. St Louis de Montfort said that if he didn't have a cross on a particular day, he felt it was because God didn't think he was strong enough.

4

Jesus Christ: the Way, the Truth, and the Life

"In many and various ways God spoke of old to our fathers by the prophets, but in these last days he has spoken to us by a Son." Christ, the Son of God made man, is the Father's one, perfect and unsurpassable Word. In him he has said everything; there will be no other word than this one. (CCC 65)

Jesus took on our nature, the nature of a slave, and all we need or desire is in Him. Those who receive Christ in their hearts are slaves become brothers—true sons of God. We can especially see the human side of Jesus in His encounter with the Samaritan woman, meditating on the fact that the Word of God felt fatigue—why did He accept tiredness? According to our way of thinking Jesus' divinity should have overwhelmed His humanity, but this did not happen.

When we do normal things it is as persons who act, and it was the same with Jesus, who was human like us, who became incarnate, but was also divine. This is a great mystery and should make us ask what exactly a person is, this focus of so many wonderful attributes. Jesus is consubstantial with the Father, begotten not created. Each action of Jesus is to be adored and admired, a way for us to nourish our faith. Marthe was not thinking in terms of theological perspectives when she emphasized all this. If we are truly united to Jesus then it is actually Him who is working or eating or sleeping in us. As we realize our membership of the Body of Christ more fully, then, according to St Thomas Aquinas, our union with Christ becomes more intimate. The *Catechism* puts it this way:

> Believers who respond to God's word and become members of Christ's Body, become intimately united with him: 'In that body the life of Christ is communicated to those who believe, and who, through the sacraments, are united in a hidden and real way to Christ in his Passion and glorification.' (CCC 790)

The Heart of Jesus contains the fullness of all virtues. Jesus is the "book of all books"—this thought was a source of great joy for Marthe. The Heart of Jesus instructs us, if we will allow Him, and helps us to accept suffering. God is present in the most intimate moments of our lives. Jesus was both God and man and so He can reveal divine things to us. The Holy Spirit lived in the heart of the Word of God.

Jesus as God, Messiah, and Man

Jesus showed His divinity by working miracles, and indeed everything about Jesus is worthy of adoration. He did all the normal things except commit sin. He fully expressed himself as a human being. Jesus was a man who needed to eat, sleep, cry—all the things we do. He had a fully human personality. God appeared in all His glory as a Man; so Jesus pulls aside the veil between us and God. The revelation of Jesus was made for all, and we must meditate on Jesus' life. Poor people often understand the mystery of Jesus much better than the rich.

St Mark's Gospel shows us Jesus as the Christ. This was the witness of the early Church; that Jesus was more than just a man and that His true nature was hidden. Even during His childhood Jesus was conscious that God was His Father. We must enter into the mystery of Christ's love—otherwise we only stay on the edge of the heart. Sometimes we allow stupid jealousies to develop in our relationships; we must examine this closely—are we really giving our best?

> Christ's whole earthly life—his words and deeds, his silences and sufferings, indeed his manner of being and speaking—is *Revelation* of the Father. Jesus can say: "Whoever has seen me has seen the Father", and the Father can say: "This is my Son, my Chosen; listen to him!" Because our Lord became man in order to do his Father's will, even the least characteristics of his mysteries manifest "God's love. . . among us". (CCC 516)

The face of Christ is an expression of the tenderness of the Father. We should never get tired of meditating on the first chapter of St Paul's letter to the Ephesians—it is Paul's Magnificat.

> Blessed be the God and Father of our Lord Jesus Christ, who has blessed us in Christ with every spiritual blessing in the heavenly places, even as he chose us in him before the foundation of the world, that we should be holy and blameless before him. He destined us in love to be his sons through Jesus Christ, according to the purpose of his will, to the praise of his glorious grace which he freely bestowed on us in the Beloved. In him we have redemption through his blood, the forgiveness of our trespasses, according to the riches of his grace which he lavished upon us.
>
> For he has made known to us in all wisdom and insight the mystery of his will, according to his purpose which he set forth in Christ as a plan for the fulness of time, to unite all things in him, things in heaven and things on earth. In him, according to the purpose of him who accomplishes all things according to the counsel of his will, we who first hoped in Christ have been destined and appointed to live for the praise of his glory. In him you also, who have heard the word of truth, the gospel of your salvation, and have believed in him, were sealed with the promised Holy Spirit, which is the guarantee of our inheritance until we acquire possession of it, to the praise of his glory. (Eph 1:3-14)

St Paul wrote the captivity epistles during his time in Rome. He was obviously overcome with the fullness of God's love.

He described the mystery of the Incarnation in terms of Jesus' subordination as man to the Father. Jesus as Savior has to be considered in His totality; we have to reflect on this with the whole of our being. The Dogmatic Constitution of the Church, *Lumen Gentium*, is based on this text from Ephesians, and its opening section is as follows:

> Christ is the Light of nations. Because this is so, this Sacred Synod gathered together in the Holy Spirit eagerly desires, by proclaiming the Gospel to every creature, to bring the light of Christ to all men, a light brightly visible on the countenance of the Church. Since the Church is in Christ like a sacrament or as a sign and instrument both of a very closely knit union with God and of the unity of the whole human race, it desires now to unfold more fully to the faithful of the Church and to the whole world its own inner nature and universal mission. This it intends to do following faithfully the teaching of previous councils. The present- day conditions of the world add greater urgency to this work of the Church so that all men, joined more closely today by various social, technical and cultural ties, might also attain fuller unity in Christ.

5

Prayer: the Absolute Priority in Life

The acts of faith, hope, and charity enjoined by the first commandment are accomplished in prayer. Lifting up the mind toward God is an expression of our adoration of God: prayer of praise and thanksgiving, intercession and petition. Prayer is an indispensable condition for being able to obey God's commandments. "[We] ought always to pray and not lose heart." (CCC 2098)

We need to rediscover the full meaning of the sign of the cross, the prayer in which we invoke Father, Son and Spirit.

To live a life of love we must offer everything—our strength to do this comes from prayer. We face the problem of how to live this life and carry out our normal tasks and responsibilities. We need prayer to cope with all our everyday problems if we are to live life properly. Our prayer is a sort of combat since our hearts so often have mixed emotions. As the soul is to the body so prayer is to life. The soul must be fed to grow—this is done through prayer. Marthe stressed the absolute need for prayer. Our life is in our own hands, and thus we have a duty to look after our soul. It is the image of God within us, containing the life of God we received at Baptism. This is our personal responsibility.

Thus we must get our priorities right—otherwise we can end up as a spiritual "desert." We must feed our soul through prayer; we have to develop the habit of looking after our spiritual life. We all need to receive inspiration through prayer, we have to develop the need to pray. But we also have to remain free and not feel as though we are forcing ourselves. We need an "open" attitude, one which leaves us free enough to pray as God wants to feed us spiritually at that moment.

Prayer must not be rushed—we should rather rejoice in the presence of God. Love works quietly. We need at least a quarter of an hour of silence with God. Then God can speak deep in our soul. The interior man lasts for ever—all other things cease. Children also need these times of quiet with God. Thus, our basic attitudes to prayer should be those of gentleness, repetition and childlike confidence. We shouldn't be too occupied but rather act as little children before God. We need to offer "small" prayers to God frequently. Work can empty us so we need to fill our lives with prayer. There is a great need for prayer, for the sick, for vocations; we need people to concentrate on the harvest.

Marthe emphasized the power of prayer before the Blessed Sacrament, the real presence of God who loves us deeply. We must sound out our souls before God in the Blessed Sacrament and listen to Him in our hearts. We should encourage others to adore Christ in the tabernacle.

We feel we are losing time by praying or giving thanks, but this is a temptation to be resisted. We shouldn't start our day without prayer. The person who prays knows their place in creation—otherwise we lose the whole meaning of our being. When a prayer has a particular purpose it becomes even more fruitful. To regret not having prayed is already a prayer, providing our regret is sincere. Prayer needs a certain structure at times; we can't always be spontaneous. We also need to put more energy into our prayer, having a particular time and place for it.

We should live within our own souls—all the divine light is there. Marthe said a day without prayer is like a day without sun or rain. So we should pray each day, even if we are busy: do what's possible, however little. We are taken by God when we pray so we shouldn't refuse a few moments with Him, and then our day will be illuminated. We are often too vague with God; our prayers must mean something and not just be words. God takes us and leads us with tenderness. Prayer isn't a luxury but a duty. As the *Catechism* puts it: "Prayer is a vital necessity. Proof from the contrary is no less convincing: if we do not allow the Spirit to lead us, we fall back into the slavery of sin. How can the Holy Spirit be our life if our heart is far from him?" (CCC 2744)

Types of Prayer

Our first duty is to adore God even if we are feeling very dry and uninspired. We should take a religious text, say a biblical passage, and just realise that God is there and that is all we need. We can thus pray to God, asking Him to have mercy on us.

Our second duty is to praise God, asking Him for the grace to open our hearts even more, being aware that His mercy and goodness are unending. We can also give thanks to God for giving us Mary, a mother of such quality.

Our third duty is that of giving thanks to God, a prayer of recognition and gratitude for all the graces we have received. We can give thanks for our parents, for our Christian education, for being born into a Christian family, for our first communion, and conversion, where these are applicable.

Our fourth duty is to make an offering of ourselves. Our meditation should make us holy. Marthe said that prayer like good works is only fertile through sacrifice. Charles de Foucauld was ready for everything, sure of God's grace, which is always given when it is required, as his prayer of abandonment indicates:

Father, I abandon myself into your hands; do with me whatever you will. Whatever you may do, I thank you: I am ready for all, I accept all. Let only your will be done in me, and in all your creatures. I wish no more than this, O Lord. Into your hands I commend my soul; I offer it to you with all the love of my heart, for I love you, Lord, and so need to give myself, to surrender myself into your hands, without reserve, and with boundless confidence, for you are my Father.

Those who seem far from God can often be closest—those who think they know God can be like the Pharisees, full of pride and self-righteousness. People who think they are safe enough through their own efforts should be careful in case they fall; they can be struck by disaster when pride makes them think they can do without God. We need to pray both for ourselves and others to prevent this. We should pray, too, for non-Christian families, pray that the spirit of Christianity may give a spiritual quality to the human virtues of those around us.

So our prayer is made up of adoration, praise, thanksgiving and offering. Prayer must be followed by a giving of self, so we need to make sacrifices of some sort. Our prayer gains quality through sacrifice. The best conversion is from good to better. We must put evil deeds behind us and move from prayer to burning prayer, and this isn't easy. We are called to be saints and the Lord has need of saints. We should write down the moments of grace in our lives and be aware of them. The Spirit chooses the right words for our prayer, taking things as they come, our feelings and ideas, and presenting them for us to God.

The Will of God

We need to read, and carefully meditate on, the following passage.

God has revealed [these things] to us through the Spirit. For the Spirit searches everything, even the depths of God. For what person knows a man's thoughts except the spirit of the man which is in him? So also no one comprehends the thoughts of God except the Spirit of God. Now we have received not the spirit of the world, but the Spirit which is from God, that we might understand the gifts bestowed on us by God. And we impart this in words not taught by human wisdom but taught by the Spirit, interpreting spiritual truths to those who possess the Spirit. The unspiritual man does not receive the gifts of the Spirit of God, for they are folly to him, and he is not able to understand them because they are spiritually discerned. The spiritual man judges all things, but is himself to be judged by no one. "For who has known the mind of the Lord so as to instruct him?" But we have the mind of Christ. (1 Cor 2:10-16)

We have to accept God's will; He won't ask us for anything which is beyond us. However, we need to be careful of making promises which are too difficult for us to keep; we have to be realistic since only the Saints can do things like that. But we must still have an infinite trust in God as our Father:

We ask our Father to unite our will to his Son's, in order to fulfill his will, his plan of salvation for the life of the world. We are radically incapable of this, but united with Jesus and with the power of his Holy Spirit, we can surrender our will to Him and decide to choose what his Son has always chosen: to do what is pleasing to the Father. (CCC 2825)

It should be very agreeable for us to do God's will. If we look for this then everything else will be given to us. We need to be wary of some pleasures and keep them at arms length. We will have the joy of being sinners who can return to God our Father. Marthe said that the charity of Jesus and Mary will reinvigorate the Church.

Martha and Mary

Now as they went on their way, he entered a village; and a woman named Martha received him into her house. And she had a sister called Mary, who sat at the Lord's feet and listened to his teaching. But Martha was distracted with much serving; and she went to him and said, "Lord, do you not care that my sister has left me to serve alone? Tell her then to help me." But the Lord answered her, "Martha, Martha, you are anxious and troubled about many things; one thing is needful. Mary has chosen the good portion, which shall not be taken away from her." (Luke 10:38-42)

Martha was doing all the cooking and preparation while Mary sat at Jesus' feet in prayer and contemplation. When a guest comes we give them a good meal, and so Martha did this when Jesus visited her house. She didn't like Mary just sitting at Jesus' feet, but in reality in Mary's heart there was a willingness, a desire to hear Jesus. The same desire was in the Virgin Mary's heart to listen to her son, even as she took care of Him and Joseph in Nazareth. She offered up her work as a prayer and we can do the same.

Listening to Jesus, as Mary did, is the better part—we too can work and pray, and indeed these two together are better than distracted prayer. We must do things in union with God, be helpful, kind; the essential thing is to love, to put love into our work. If we do things with care and from the heart then we are combining the best of Martha and Mary. St Paul spoke of the hard work involved in running our race towards God. So we need to pace ourselves, choosing a suitable rhythm and scheme of prayer. Martha and Mary both had something to give, but Jesus didn't reproach Martha for working, rather because she wasn't taking time to look outside herself. We can feel we are like Martha, working hard, with everyone else relaxing—this is something which can particularly affect parents.

So we have to live the present moment, in love. This means spending a lot of time in prayer to understand our role in the world, to be the leaven in the dough. Jesus said Mary had chosen the better part in the more open attitude of her heart, and He advised Martha to do the same. We have to be in contact with Jesus' heart no matter what we do. Our task is to work hard for the food which will never perish; we head towards our goal—that of reaching God, full of desire and without laziness, understanding that everyone needs to do work of some sort. It doesn't matter that we haven't actually seen Christ—He is present all around us in the poor and sick. Martha shows us the attitude we should have towards the corporal works of mercy, but Mary shows us the interior attitude we need.

6

Silence, Meditation, and Contemplation

The hidden life at Nazareth allows everyone to enter into fellowship with Jesus by the most ordinary events of daily life: The home of Nazareth is the school where we begin to understand the life of Jesus—the school of the Gospel. First, then, a lesson of silence. May esteem for silence, that admirable and indispensable condition of mind, revive in us. (CCC 533)

The spirit of silence is important since the noise of the world can have an adverse effect on us. With silence we can respond from the heart to life's problems, and it is necessary to discover the deep needs of the soul. Time for reflection is also important: our life could end today. We must meet the conditions necessary to live life more deeply and fully. This means letting the "interior voice" develop in quietness and peace. Thus we must discover the voice of our soul. For this to happen we mustn't already be full of the world. Silence is indispensable for more profound ideas to surface.

Perhaps we could have silence at work instead of listening to the radio? This would give us an opportunity for prayer during the day. We can pray for those we work with, but need to be careful of speaking about "religion," that is putting it into the realm of the extraordinary rather than the ordinary. We should offer up our daily work to God. Marthe's prayer, the fruit of her silence, was an intimate talk with God, an intimate "commerce," or exchange, or friendship, with God. Marthe said we should look to Mary who kept the word in her heart. In sum, we need to understand the value of silence if we are to really hear God.

Meditation & Contemplation

The spiritual writers, paraphrasing Matthew 7:7, summarize in this way the dispositions of the heart nourished by the Word of God in prayer: "Seek in reading and you will find in meditating; knock in mental prayer and it will be opened to you by contemplation." (CCC 2654)

We have to go down into the very heart of our soul—we mustn't stay on the edge of our being. When reading or meditating on Scripture we need to stay with the text to understand and assimilate it. We mustn't be closed to God, but open and present. This takes time but is necessary since nothing worthwhile develops overnight. Marthe discovered the need to go into the deep interior of the soul to reflect, meditate and work. We "work" in God's presence in meditating on the Scriptures, deep inside the self. Contemplation is a human action. It is, or should be, the principal action of man—the reason for our creation:

What is contemplative prayer? St. Teresa answers: 'Contemplative prayer in my opinion is nothing else than a close sharing between friends; it means taking time frequently to be alone with him who we know loves us.' (CCC 2709)

Contemplation is the essential thing. God can change us to the extent we are open to His action in our soul. We must free our interior attraction for God. Even children can contemplate and there can be a deep level of contemplation between mother and child. Our deep attraction for God will develop as our life of prayer develops. We can't rely too much on reason; rather we should be looking for a light from God which will change our life.

In reality, a true contemplative has to be someone who believes in the Trinity and so contemplation can only really exist in Christianity, despite the good points found in Eastern religions. This means that those Christians who embrace Eastern religious practises don't really understand the Trinity; their faith isn't sufficiently well grounded.

We need to read the Scriptures and meditate on them so as to come to a full identification with the Cross. When meditating we shouldn't concentrate on the historical or exegetical aspects of Scripture. We must rather see it as food for our souls, the Word of God. Our hearts need to be nourished. As the *Catechism* says:

> In Sacred Scripture, the Church constantly finds her nourishment and her strength, for she welcomes it not as a human word, 'but as what it really is, the word of God'. 'In the sacred books, the Father who is in heaven comes lovingly to meet his children, and talks with them.' (CCC 104)

Our understanding of Scripture isn't due to the intellectual side alone; but regrettably a true sense of Scripture is lacking amongst many Christians today. Scripture is inspired—each word is important and the Church is the only authentic interpreter of Scripture, such that she, "forcefully and specifically exhorts all the Christian faithful ... to learn the surpassing knowledge of Jesus Christ, by frequent reading of the divine Scriptures. Ignorance of the Scriptures is ignorance of Christ." (CCC 133)

Jacob wrestles with God

> The same night he arose and took his two wives, his two maids, and his eleven children, and crossed the ford of the Jabbok. He took them and sent them across the stream, and likewise everything that he had. And Jacob was left alone ... (Gen 32:22-24)

Jacob was left alone and struggled to discover his mission. When we come to Church we should enter into the mystery of Christ, otherwise it's pointless going. We mustn't stop at exterior aspects but enter into the mystery. The truth opens people's minds. Without an interior life we won't know how to act. We must look within, at a deeper level and not just at the easy things on the surface. It isn't a question of "methods" but rather of entering into our own hearts in silence and love.

... and a man wrestled with him until the breaking of the day. When the man saw that he did not prevail against Jacob, he touched the hollow of his thigh; and Jacob's thigh was put out of joint as he wrestled with him. Then he said, "Let me go, for the day is breaking." But Jacob said, "I will not let you go, unless you bless me." And he said to him, "What is your name?" And he said, "Jacob." Then he said, "Your name shall no more be called Jacob, but Israel, for you have striven with God and with men, and have prevailed."

Then Jacob asked him, "Tell me, I pray, your name." But he said, "Why is it that you ask my name?" And there he blessed him. So Jacob called the name of the place Peniel, saying, "For I have seen God face to face, and yet my life is preserved." The sun rose upon him as he passed Penuel, limping because of his thigh. Therefore to this day the Israelites do not eat the sinew of the hip which is upon the hollow of the thigh, because he touched the hollow of Jacob's thigh on the sinew of the hip. (Gen 32:24-32)

Jacob was in agony before God, wounded in the struggle with God. It is also difficult for us to accept "combat" with God for the graces and helps we need. A deep need within us for the presence of God is what really matters. We should start from that part of Scripture which really touches and inspires us. Thus we mustn't live on the edge of our powers, we must enter into His presence. We can go to Mass, pray and so on, but not get into the depths of our potential; we must avoid making it all a matter of routine. The dependable, reliable person goes deep down into the heart, reflects on God's Word and becomes calm. We need to really enter into ourselves to fully develop and flower. It is very important to have a point to dwell or meditate on. God wants souls which are on fire— not people stifled by learning.

Contemplation is from the Heart

There is a definite difference between meditation and contemplation. Meditation is God's gift where He speaks to us, through Scripture, for example. Contemplation is the will to give the mind to God—but not in a passive or easy way; it involves an intimate conversation. God works on the soul and gives us an aptitude of heart. Meditation is a reflection on the gift of God, in which we use our minds. Contemplation is more of the heart.

We must contemplate the beauty and greatness of Mary. When meditating we should let the text sink in, and have the attitude of Mary who kept everything in her heart and pondered all that she had seen. We shouldn't rush around unnecessarily but instead spend time on the things of God. So we need to meditate on these things and make them a part of our heart and mind. The ordinary things are the most important as exemplified in Marthe's love and humility. We should think about the love of God who died for us. We find this difficult to accept and believe—there is too much action and not enough adoration in our lives:

> Adoration is the first act of the virtue of religion. To adore God is to acknowledge him as God, as the Creator and Saviour, the Lord and Master of everything that exists, as infinite and merciful Love. 'You shall worship the Lord your God, and him only shall you serve,' says Jesus, citing Deuteronomy. (CCC 2096)

By an act of faith in the presence of God we believe something is in us which is greater than anything we can see. When we meditate, we should prepare properly and make sure we have things straight in our own minds, and not just depend on our feelings. We have to think, penetrate, question—what does God want of us? We need to concentrate on the text we are meditating on: it's too easy to stay outside the text without really entering into it.

Spiritual Reading

It is good to read spiritual books by authors such as Dom Marmion, the Benedictine; we should cultivate ourselves, but not get overloaded. We can't be active Christians if we only have a superficial knowledge of our faith. So delve deep and begin to adore, begin to be united to the heart of God. Perhaps there would be fewer suicides if more people knew they were loved from all eternity in the heart of God. People haven't understood because they haven't thought about it— we have to work at all this and keep coming back to the text.

Each of us has his own particular nature, so develop naturally—those who have been back to the sources are the real educators; we mustn't be imitators but must be creative. Everything is to be included in Christ: we can't read the history of the Church or the accounts of the martyrs unless we have a reverential attitude—we aren't reading a novel. So we need to read the text on our knees, figuratively speaking; this was the attitude of Marthe— it isn't just a question of exegesis or analysis.

Reading the Scriptures

God the Holy Spirit is the author of Sacred Scripture. "The divinely revealed realities, which are contained and presented in the text of Sacred Scripture, have been written down under the inspiration of the Holy Spirit." (CCC 105)

Similarly, our reading of Scripture should be structured— don't give in to spiritual curiosity, don't flit from one text to another. When we meditate we need to enter into a text in depth. We mustn't read the Word of God like a newspaper, rather it requires calm and conviction. Thus, our nourishment should come from the Bible, and we mustn't see a true understanding of it as something just for scholars and intellectuals. The Word of God should structure our being as true men and women: if we carry on as before in a servile way, then we haven't really heard the Word of God. This Word must enter deeply into us—not just into memory or mind. We are meant to bear fruit that will last.

It is often hard to assimilate biblical texts, especially for those who are ill, but the effort must be made. Such an effort demands energy but we are lazy and tend to stay at the threshold when we should go further. Children often have a fresher and more open attitude to the Scriptures. These texts come from the heart of God and the Word of God in the Bible is to be venerated—it is not just another book.

God has given us the extraordinary gift of the Scriptures, and we must be careful to attentively study the biblical text, which gives us the key to all the great scriptural events of the past. The deeper meaning of the Scriptures only comes through the heart, through prayer; the accounts we read there should inspire us to greater efforts. They contain the foundation of our faith, and so we must read and study them. Thus, we have to be careful in our choice of books for both prayer and study, and our spiritual food by preference should be the Scriptures. As Catholics we have work to do; it is essential that we know the Scriptures, as *Dei Verbum* and other documents from the Second Vatican Council tell us.

When reading a passage of Scripture, especially when Jesus is mentioned, we should concentrate on the verbs used, on the human activities. All the actions of Jesus mentioned in the Gospel belong to the person of the Word, the second person of the Trinity, someone who is God but also man; He eats, walks, sleeps, and so on, and in honoring all these human actions we also pay homage to the divine. We should stop and consider all this, admire and adore; this was St. Augustine's method. God predestined us, in advance, to be in the heart of Christ. We should ask Marthe to enlighten us as to the meaning of that. We will lose our way on occasion, but this doesn't mean we are wasting our time, despite temptations.

We should take and search, not being over-concerned with the words, telling the Lord of our poverty, and being prepared to be quiet and to listen. The reason why true contemplatives don't get tired is that they don't need relaxation in the heart of God. We need to meditate on God's mercy, and be renewed every day; we shouldn't dwell too much on the future but rather on God's infinite mercy. Ask for God's mercy and forgiveness—don't fear, only believe.

7

Humility, Discernment, Detachment, & the Desire for God

We mustn't be like the hypocrites who parade their good qualities before others; but nowadays our hypocrisy is turned inwards, towards ourselves: we become self-satisfied and pharisaical, saying we aren't as bad as everyone else. We try to show others only our good points.

We need humility to ask for forgiveness. Jesus lived in poverty and made himself humble. We should also be humble and lean on God, and so be raised up from our nothingness. We need to think about these things in our hearts. Jesus, like us, lived in an ordinary state. He had to work hard for a living and get on with the people of Nazareth. The humility of Our Lady gives us a model we can imitate.

We must contemplate Christ born among us in humility and ordinariness. We should be drawn to Christ's lowliness in being born in a stable in poverty: we mustn't dehumanize Jesus as though He didn't experience the problems of life. We should be conscious of our humanity and poverty, so we can give ourselves to others. This is the reason for our creation—to make an offering of ourselves, to love. We must give our hearts back to God. The poverty of the Cross demands that we take the last place. Thus, we should all cultivate humility, especially as we grow older.

The desire to forgive is in the heart of God—but how can we forgive like God? We always feel we have done enough. We see true forgiveness in the lives of people like St Maximilian Kolbe, who endured the bestiality of the concentration camp at Auschwitz. He took the place of another prisoner in a punishment cell and was the last to survive starvation, until he was killed by injection. Yet despite His sufferings, like Christ, he showed amazing forgiveness. The same was true of Marthe who endured her own terrible sufferings in union with Jesus, and yet was still prepared to listen to the problems of those who came to see her. We are acting as true Christians when we can forgive.

Discernment

Each person has to find his or her place in the world, but it is often difficult for us, as sinners, to see this. We have to put our lives in order and discover the essentials. This means being audacious in the practise of our faith, whether it is in celibacy or in parents looking after their children. We don't always understand each other and need a sense of direction rather like homing pigeons, who circle around until they have found the right way. We have our own journey to make to God and while we need to rest, we shouldn't stop or hesitate unduly: we can sometimes become obstinate or cease to search. However, it's essential to continue to look, as we realise deep down that the fullness of life isn't in us—we need God.

We should reflect and help others to reflect; this involves a disciplining of the mind, but we shouldn't be afraid to go beyond what we feel are the limits of our strength: we will always be helped sufficiently and can never really do enough for God anyway. It is very necessary for us to channel our thoughts effectively, otherwise we are not acting in a fully human manner. We need to take time to meditate, to really understand things. But we should beware of ideas which come quickly to mind—they are probably due to sentiment or feeling. So reflection is important; we should really think about what we wish to do.

As the *Catechism* says:

> ... man recognizes the voice of God which urges him 'to do what is good and avoid what is evil.' Everyone is obliged to follow this law, which makes itself heard in conscience and is fulfilled in the love of God and of neighbor. Living a moral life bears witness to the dignity of the person. (1706)

Regarding this question of discernment, St Ignatius of Loyola's exercises are a different sort of teaching from Marthe's; but there are also many similarities. Ignatius reflected on a book given to him about the life of Christ. He asked himself if he could compete with St Francis and St Dominic. Ignatius lived at the time of new ideas, a time of achievement and so he too felt he could achieve something, both for himself and in helping others to "discern the spirits." He felt happy with earthly thoughts initially, but once they were over, he felt dry and discontented. Conversely, the stories of the saints gave him consolation at the time, and he also felt at peace after his meditations. The discernment of spirits is based on this difference. Gradually, Ignatius came to realise the difference between worldly and spiritual sadness, and joy. This was a more profound spiritual discovery than a psychological one; something at a deeper level than just feelings or emotions. So Ignatius gradually realised the different types of spirit that were moving him.

After we have discerned what we think we should do, we need to ask practical questions—is the action we propose practical and can we actually do it? We mustn't push things to excess however, we need to keep a balance and not overlook the role of the intellect. We shouldn't make decisions in one go; it takes some time to know what is right. Decisions need to have depth, otherwise it's like putting paint on rotten wood.

Detachment

The precept of detachment from riches is obligatory for entrance into the Kingdom of heaven. ... Abandonment to the providence of the Father in heaven frees us from anxiety about tomorrow. Trust in God is a preparation for the blessedness of the poor. They shall see God. ... Desire for true happiness frees man from his immoderate attachment to the goods of this world so that he can find his fulfillment in the vision and beatitude of God. (CCC 2544, 2547-48)

Marthe was very attached to everyday life, to the farm and the animals. She had enjoyed the social life of the farm and the village, and had to give all this up as she became more paralyzed. We should prize and enjoy everyday things but not get too strongly attached to anything except God.

If we fully consecrate ourselves to God then the desire in us for material things lessens. We are then free to give our hearts to God in a spirit of great love. This is only really understood by those who have known and lived it. We must live in the world without taking our inspirations from it. The world has only a relative value: we need to be detached from it so we can be free to serve God. Jesus tells us to ask for anything and we shall receive it. He instructs our hearts and strengthens our commitment to Him, asking us to follow Him in simplicity as the first disciples did.

We need, then, to be determined to remove the things which stop us from reaching God, particularly our own evil-minded inclinations, as well as those of other people. We need to have a certain "hatred" for anything which would take us from God. This means overcoming obstacles and not just accepting them as inevitable, as something we cannot master: we must put them aside as necessary. We must ask God to know our hearts and watch over us, leading us on the path of eternity.

So we can't compromise our religious ideals if we want eternal life; we mustn't continue to run after material things, just accumulating money; this is something we have to understand. However, having said that, we also have to look after the material side of life and be prepared to work and cultivate, to produce the necessities of life. This is not a recipe for laziness.

The man who doesn't let himself be corrected by God is very unfortunate. In all this, we have to stay near Jesus in the Blessed Sacrament, telling Him our problems.

Thus, we must look at all earthly things in a heavenly light; how we live, what we give to the poor—as much as we can afford is the ideal. It isn't necessary to change one's car too often and we could cut down on holidays and give away the money saved. Don't wait for the right spiritual "feeling"— make a commitment now to help those less well off. Our lives should be marked by abstinence as we overcome pride, avarice and the other effects of original sin. We should really be dead to all this through Baptism.

We have the principle of divine life is us, hidden in our hearts and we are in the heart of the Trinity. We need to develop enthusiasm and a consciousness of how our life is hidden in God, so we can perform our earthly duties with more love.

Desire for God

The desire for God is written in the human heart, because man is created by God and for God; and God never ceases to draw man to himself. Only in God will he find the truth and happiness he never stops searching for ... "Let the hearts of those who seek the Lord rejoice." Although man can forget God or reject him, He never ceases to call every man to seek him, so as to find life and happiness. But this search for God demands of man every effort of intellect, a sound will, "an upright heart", as well as the witness of others who teach him to seek God. (CCC 27, 30)

We must develop an "attraction" for God and for others—this is a grace we should pray for every day. But we must also develop the sensitivity to accept others as they are. This attraction of the heart leads us to God. We must ask Jesus for the grace to have an attraction for God, using Mary as our model. Our spirit is "bathed" in God. This attraction for God is innate in small children, but it still needs to be developed. The soul needs God. Wanting God doesn't stop us being in the reality of life but we do need times of silence, since God speaks to us mainly in stillness and quiet.

The attraction for money, sensuality, the pride of life—all of these can develop in us, so preventing the attraction for God. How can the sheep resist the attack of the wolf?—we must have a burning love. The important thing is an ardent desire in our hearts; without this there is no ardor in life. Thus we need to go to the source of this ardor. Why does the Father want to invite men to help in redemption? Because, amongst other things, it leads to the joy of fruitfulness in our lives. This was the work of Jesus; we must have this ardor in our life or everything becomes mechanical. Don't look for a "method" in all this.

All of us have a want or desire in our heart for God; we are creatures in the process of becoming, of reaching our full potential. So we must develop our desire with gentleness and be careful to realise our limitations, and where our gifts and abilities lie, and especially that God is the source of any talents we may have. So we have to have our roots in a good soil, and this entails a desire for fulfilment which reaches its goal in God. God's tenderness and love for us are seen in the face of Christ, with Mary His Mother. We need to go slowly and securely to them, but in a straight line, like St Paul.

We must, then, become aware of this fundamental desire in us for God, and learn how to perceive this desire correctly. Our job is to develop this desire, since we are made for God. Our perception of this desire depends on our individual makeup; so we have to see how we can correspond more closely in our daily life with this hidden desire for God.

The angels help us in ordinary life particularly our guardian angels; they are living beings we should pray to. Our guardian angel is our go-between who intercedes for us with God, and puts us in touch with the Holy Spirit. He helps us and we should love him, he is God's messenger for us. We also need Mary's help; she is our sweet Mother. We need to move towards God, forgetting created things, trying to truly discover God. We are in God's hands and should rest in His love.

To discover God demands an ascetic attitude; one of prayer, of going to Mass, of adopting certain disciplined practices. These should never, though, become automatic. We have to be moderate in our enjoyment of comfort. This involves us praying more, doing without food and sleep; we need to approach Jesus on our knees. There is a need for abstinence, a disciplining of the mouth and stomach, but it shouldn't be exaggerated. Abstinence is liberating, but it must be free and not forced on people. We can be like the Pharisees and prone to exaggeration—but this doesn't mean rejecting the good things which came out of the mentality of the Old Testament: Jesus, Mary, Joseph, Simeon, Anna, Joachim and Anne all came from this atmosphere.

How can we represent the phenomenon of the beatific vision, the clear sight of God? We must work towards this as our goal and it can't be done without effort. We must run in order to get the prize. This means killing our earthly desires, our anger and other passions. Instead, we should be kind and compassionate, forgiving others and looking for the inspiration of the Spirit in our lives and worship. St Paul gave the extraordinary advice to never do anything except in Christ. If we do this, the hidden seed in us will be revealed when we are resurrected.

Jesus has an intense desire to live in us, a desire which is infinitely greater than our own desires. He is waiting for us, to feed us, to transform us. So we can "recreate" our personal unity with His help wherever we are. But we have to fight against our human weakness, our tendency towards evil and the desire for comfort. We can spend too much time sleeping, or talking and chatting. Despite this, God is always active in our lives. We can benefit from the inactivity which comes through illness, giving ourselves up to suffering, a process in which we are helped by God's grace. Marthe's whole life teaches us this important point.

The Parable of the Sower

Hear then the parable of the sower. When any one hears the word of the kingdom and does not understand it, the evil one comes and snatches away what is sown in his heart; this is what was sown along the path. As for what was sown on rocky ground, this is he who hears the word and immediately receives it with joy; yet he has no root in himself, but endures for a while, and when tribulation or persecution arises on account of the word, immediately he falls away. As for what was sown among thorns, this is he who hears the word, but the cares of the world and the delight in riches choke the word, and it proves unfruitful. As for what was sown on good soil, this is he who hears the word and understands it; he indeed bears fruit, and yields, in one case a hundredfold, in another sixty, and in another thirty. (Matt 13:18-23)

We should ask the Holy Spirit to help us understand the parable of the sower. God's garden was the land of Israel, but when He came to gather its fruit it was devastated. When Jesus comes into our hearts the thorns and stones are there in abundance. He wants us to tend our own garden, to remove the obstacles in the way of really coming to know Him. We should be able to give thanks to the Lord that the land has been turned over enough for Him to plant His goodness in us: if there are any thorns or weeds left they will stifle the Word of God, and thus we just can't go on feelings or appearances. It takes courage for us to remove these since it is much easier to leave them there, but with help we can remove them, if we cooperate with grace.

When we meditate on the Stations of the Cross we can consider the state of our lives with respect to the love shown in Christ's sacrifice. His blood and sweat were the result of our sin; we must work to regain our hearts and remove the thorns and the root of evil in us. Jesus tore His hands and His head on these thorns. The body we receive in the Eucharist is not only risen but also still bleeding, figuratively, because of our sins. Jesus is put back into the rock of the tomb, into our pride, instead of into the depths of our hearts. After the rock of our heart has been split open, Jesus is the gardener who will work on it and prepare a place for himself. But we have to help by opening our hearts fully to Him. This work cost the sweat and blood of a God. So we must be full of gratitude, and should pray about this, so as to be able to really see what He has done for each of us.

8

Children of God
& Brothers of Christ

He who believes in Christ becomes a son of God. This filial adoption transforms him by giving him the ability to follow the example of Christ. It makes him capable of acting rightly and doing good. In union with his Saviour, the disciple attains the perfection of charity which is holiness. Having matured in grace, the moral life blossoms into eternal life in the glory of heaven. (CCC 1709)

We are blessed and chosen—destined to be God's adoptive son's. How is it that these words which are so strong mean so little to us? We are, when in a state of grace, joyful temples of the Holy Spirit, of the Trinitarian Life within us. Everything will be recapitulated in Christ. The most important thing is for us to integrate our faith with our life. We shouldn't be mechanical, since faith and actions go together. If people's hearts aren't in it then their actions aren't truly human.

We are blessed, holy and graced with the love of God which flows through the Church. The Trinitarian life of believers is based on the principle that the Father has intended we should become adopted sons through Jesus Christ. We are limited creatures with limited understanding—we are sinners and ignorant. It's possible for people to know a lot of things and yet not know the real reason for their lives. Jesus has revealed all this to us. Human beings have a heart to love; this is the difference between us and the animals—we are children of God. The following parable of Jesus tells us who we are and who God is.

The "Prodigal" Son

There was a man who had two sons; and the younger of them said to his father, "Father, give me the share of property that falls to me." And he divided his living between them. Not many days later, the younger son gathered all he had and took his journey into a far country, and there he squandered his property in loose living. And when he had spent everything, a great famine arose in that country, and he began to be in want. So he went and joined himself to one of the citizens of that country, who sent him into his fields to feed swine. And he would gladly have fed on the pods that the swine ate; and no one gave him anything.

But when he came to himself he said, "How many of my father's hired servants have bread enough and to spare, but I perish here with hunger! I will arise and go to my father, and I will say to him, 'Father, I have sinned against heaven and before you; I am no longer worthy to be called your son; treat me as one of your hired servants.' " And he arose and came to his father. (Luke 15:11-20)

We need to take part in the feeling of this parable. We are created as sons of the Father—created as God's children. A child has inheritance rights and resembles its father, that is, we are like God, we are made in His image and likeness. We should meditate to receive the Spirit so we can become fully aware of this fact, that we are sons of God. We need an open heart to fully believe this. Because we are "sons" with inheritance rights we are able to demand our "heritage." We can choose to go against God and sin. But if we are honest we can't just treat God as a distributor of things and be constantly saying to Him "give me." We must give back to God what we receive.

Sin is separation from God as our Creator and Father. There is a parallel here with our earthly parents. We must be sensitive to sin so as to be right with God. Our behavior towards God must be filial; when we achieve this we are liberated in heart.

The father divided his fortune—God respects our decisions as individuals. This is the mystery of free will. Despite the fact that we can misuse it, it is still a marvelous thing. God respects our freedom, even when we use it to offend Him. Don't go off to a far country; stay close to God; in other words we need to contemplate every day to avoid serious sin. We should go to God like children in trust. Confession to a Priest will reach us as sinners. Man's heart needs to be warmed—so we must stay close to God through prayer and meditation.

Be aware of the limitations of earthly goods—they aren't eternal. The love of God as our Father reaches us even if we are far away. Sufferings can be a warning to us that we need to withdraw into ourselves and seek God. It is difficult to get into God's kingdom if we are too rich—in money, intelligence, and other worldly goods. Failure can be beneficial, but perhaps not when it happens too often! When a person strays from God it usually leads to suffering; this can be the way we are jolted.

> But while he was yet at a distance, his father saw him and had compassion, and ran and embraced him and kissed him. And the son said to him, "Father, I have sinned against heaven and before you; I am no longer worthy to be called your son." But the father said to his servants, "Bring quickly the best robe, and put it on him; and put a ring on his hand, and shoes on his feet; and bring the fatted calf and kill it, and let us eat and make merry; for this my son was dead, and is alive again; he was lost, and is found." And they began to make merry. (Luke 15:20-24)

There are many problems in the world, problems such as the desire to dominate or succeed. But God is Father and always manages to give us what we need. He allows these problems in our lives because He has given us His Mother to care for us.

The Prodigal Son decided to repent and expiate his sins. The Father was anxiously looking for him. He had never stopped thinking about him. When he does meet him he takes pity on him and tenderly embraces him. We need to meditate on all this which is symbolic of God's care and concern for us.

> Now his elder son was in the field; and as he came and drew near to the house, he heard music and dancing. And he called one of the servants and asked what this meant. And he said to him, "Your brother has come, and your father has killed the fatted calf, because he has received him safe and sound." But he was angry and refused to go in. His father came out and entreated him, but he answered his father, "Lo, these many years I have served you, and I never disobeyed your command; yet you never gave me a kid, that I might make merry with my friends. But when this son of yours came, who has devoured your living with harlots, you killed for him the fatted calf!" And he said to him, "Son, you are always with me, and all that is mine is yours. It was fitting to make merry and be glad, for this your brother was dead, and is alive; he was lost, and is found."(Luke 15:25-32)

We need to get into the Father's heart. The emphasis should be on the father's love and not on legal things; the other son is probably guilty of this. The father tells the older son that his brother has returned, he gives him back his sense of fraternity: it is difficult for us to love each other unless we have the same Father.

Children of God

The whole aim of the Christian Life is to make us children of God, at God's right hand. The Church should be a brotherly institution, with all her children united together. We must really know and believe that we are CHILDREN OF GOD and that He really believes in and loves us. To be a child of God means to be someone who cares for our brothers and sisters. Children of the same Father shouldn't fight or quarrel. We must taste the mystery of the Church and really come to know the fullness of God, His infinity, this great mystery which is given to such limited people. Our mission is to bring people slowly and gently to God. St Paul put it this way:

> So if there is any encouragement in Christ, any incentive of love, any participation in the Spirit, any affection and sympathy, complete my joy by being of the same mind, having the same love, being in full accord and of one mind. Do nothing from selfishness or conceit, but in humility count others better than yourselves. Let each of you look not only to his own interests, but also to the interests of others.
>
> Have this mind among yourselves, which is yours in Christ Jesus, who, though he was in the form of God, did not count equality with God a thing to be grasped, but emptied himself, taking the form of a servant, being born in the likeness of men. And being found in human form he humbled himself and became obedient unto death, even death on a cross. Therefore God has highly exalted him and bestowed on him the name which is above every name, that at the name of Jesus every knee should bow, in heaven and on earth and under the earth, and every tongue confess that Jesus Christ is Lord, to the glory of God the Father. (Phil 2:1-11)

Fr Finet said that we are sons of God through the tenderness of the Father. We are adopted sons in the image of His Son. In Galatians, Paul said a son is someone who says "Abba"—Father, Dad—it is wonderful if we can speak to God like this and mean it. The nature of man is to be a son and to have a father. In the Spirit we should be making a cry of love to our Father. God's adoption of us as sons is much closer than an earthly adoption, since we are divinized by this adoption. A human child, after its adoption, doesn't assume the same nature as its new father; but we are divinized by sanctifying grace and the divine life has definite effects on us:

Filial adoption, in making us partakers by grace in the divine nature, can bestow true merit on us as a result of God's gratuitous justice. This is our right by grace, the full right of love, making us 'co-heirs' with Christ and worthy of obtaining 'the promised inheritance of eternal life.' (CCC 2009)

We are predestined to become adoptive sons and so we should act out this truth. The divine life is actually in us—we have the same life as that of the Father when we are in a state of grace. God respects His creatures and so He doesn't absorb us, but rather completes us in a divine way. We all need to understand and perceive this. We shouldn't fear God's greatness, as Pascal the French philosopher did. A dimension of us has existed from all eternity in the mind of God.

9

The Fatherhood of God: the Holy Trinity

Jesus revealed that God is Father in an unheard-of sense: he is Father not only in being Creator; he is eternally Father in relation to his only Son, who is eternally Son only in relation to his Father: 'No one knows the Son except the Father, and no one knows the Father except the Son and any one to whom the Son chooses to reveal him.' (CCC 240)

We have to purify our own idea of Fatherhood. God's Fatherhood is radical and fundamental to His being; so the Father can't be thought of without the Son. God's paternity is fully accomplished in the Son—He can't beget any other— the Son is the only Son; Jesus is the only begotten Son and there can't be more than one. So we can begin to see the need for a Trinity. In the Trinity, there is a specific order of generation without addition or subtraction. No other relationships than those of Father, Son and Spirit are possible in the Trinity.

Fatherhood on earth is the greatest reflection of the Godhead—both for human fathers and for Priests. The more they are "father" the better they are. Marthe said we should encourage fatherhood in our Priests and Bishops. If a Priest is cut off from his Bishop then he becomes spiritually sterile. For Marthe, God was the absolute "Father," a Fatherhood which also included perfect "motherhood," too, perfect concern and perfect caring. Jesus revealed this absolute Fatherhood of God, that the Father and Son do not exist without each other: this is something we can only marvel at. Jesus spoke about the Father continually, and at the Last Supper affirmed that the person who saw Him also saw the Father (John 14:9). We have to realize God's great love for us in this gift of His Son.

The Greatness of God

St Augustine spoke of the greatness and gentleness of the Father. We can also reach people more productively through gentleness and kindness, but we will face opposition. We need to love people with the sort of love Jesus would have given them. Augustine lamented having loved God so late in life, but we don't ever need to really worry about this since God is the ultimate cause of everything that happens. This is brought out in Psalm 139, which describes the way God knows every intimate detail of our lives.

This psalm shows us the way God knows everything about us and the difficulties we have in reaching Him by our own efforts. Actually, though, He is everywhere, leading and guiding us. God formed us in our mother's womb—we are a wonderful creation and everything about us was defined even before we came into being.

We can't understand God as though He is an object that can be analysed or fully explained; He is beyond us. But we can see the action of God in ourselves and our fellow men and women. The world has come from God, from His power: but there is an infinite distinction between the world and God: creation is difficult to grasp and understand. We can't see what God does in us, His scrutiny of us. He knows us more than we know ourselves. God is there—and that should be sufficient for us. He formed us and wove us; we should thank Him for the marvel of our lives. God is working constantly in us, but we mustn't cut Him short, we need His help to keep us from evil. We should be enthusiastic for God, changing our lives and rejecting evil with a holy hatred of sin.

I saw the Lord standing beside the altar, and he said: "Smite the capitals until the thresholds shake, and shatter them on the heads of all the people; and what are left of them I will slay with the sword; not one of them shall flee away, not one of them shall escape. "Though they dig into Sheol, from there shall my hand take them; though they climb up to heaven, from there I will bring them down. Though they hide themselves on the top of Carmel, from there I will search out and take them; and though they hide from my sight at the bottom of the sea, there I will command the serpent, and it shall bite them. And though they go into captivity before their enemies, there I will command the sword, and it shall slay them; and I will set my eyes upon them for evil and not for good." (Amos 9:1-4)

Amos saw the Lord upright before the altar, speaking of a stiff-necked people provoking God's anger. He would attack them and seek them out to kill them, because they had rejected Him and become selfish. Neither can we mock God with the way we live. We face the terrible modern phenomenon of people who are seen as worthless by others. We can see all the poverty in the Third World—we just can't accept things as they are. God can't be happy with all this: while the rich want to get richer still, God's anger at all this injustice is shown to us in the book of the Apocalypse. In trying to make ourselves sensitive to God's presence we face the problem of dealing with the evil both within ourselves and in the world. God is patient; He waits for us and gives us the sacraments to help us.

The Most Holy Trinity

The mystery of the Most Holy Trinity is the central mystery of Christian faith and life. It is the mystery of God in himself. It is therefore the source of all the other mysteries of faith, the light that enlightens them. It is the most fundamental and essential teaching in the "hierarchy of the truths of faith". ... The Trinity is a mystery of faith in the strict sense, one of the "mysteries that are hidden in God, which can never be known unless they are revealed by God". (CCC 234, 237)

The Holy Trinity is living as three persons in our heart, who are joined to our spirit to make us like Christ. The Father sends the Spirit through the Son as we receive sanctifying grace; we are not directly aware of this but accept it by faith. We need calm and silence to become really aware of all this; we need to take time to realize this indwelling of the Trinity which stimulates and strengthens us. Christ prays in us to the Father, and this is why we start our prayer, "In the name of the Father..."

Christian prayer should be glowing—fully aware of the immensity of God. A baptised Christian is united with the Trinity in adoring the Father and discovering Christ through the Spirit. We need to unite our own personal sacrifice with that of Jesus, so the indwelling of the Trinity within us becomes a living, dynamic exchange of love. The effects of this are very profound and very deep. We can use our memory, reasoning and imagination to go deeper and realize that we are made in God's image, and indelibly marked by Baptism. We reflect the divine presence in the world. God is in our deepest depths, the Holy Spirit is in our hearts and we live in and through Jesus, so that the Father gives us knowledge of how to live the Christian life. We have to let this life work in us—the world needs to discover Christ through us.

The incensing of the congregation during Mass is a recognition that we are all indwelt by the Holy Trinity. Similarly, funeral liturgies recognize this indwelling and the resurrection of the body on the last day. Our contact with others should recognize this indwelling, that our brothers and sisters are also marked and called by the Holy Spirit to a fuller life. There is a big difference between feeling this and knowing it interiorly, something which we can only realize as a fruit of prayer.

We should base our Christian lives on this knowledge, that other people are called to eternal life too. So there is no place for animosity, and a truly Christian life should kill off such feelings. People who upset us or make us angry may also carry the Blessed Trinity in their hearts. We need to pray that we will be able to deal with those who cause us problems. Despite this knowledge we don't change or accept this quickly; we tend to draw back instead of making the small changes to our way of life which will gradually transform us. Our faith should thus be Trinitarian, otherwise we are missing a great deal. In spite of our difficulty in understanding this, we have to make an effort.

It was pleasing to God to present the mystery of the Trinity to us as a family; we need to interiorize what the spirit of a family really means. We need points we can relate our thinking to. Jesus revealed the intimacy of the Trinity to men gradually: He didn't speak of the Spirit immediately. The Holy Spirit working in our hearts will show us how to act— we have our part to play. The fine details of God's plan pass us by, but we must try to catch what we can.

Our faith is in the mystery of the Trinity—so we can offer everything to the Three Persons, all our hopes and aspirations. We pray to the Father, "Our Father." Jesus spoke of God as "Him," His Father. But the Father is not superior to the Son. The mystery of the Trinity in revelation comes from Jesus. There are those who live in that intimacy, that faith, in a spirit of togetherness and family, and that too is our task. This "Spirit" in the Trinity is actually a person. The Holy Spirit is also a "He." The spirit of a family is different and is due to the interaction between the members and, of course, the grace of the Holy Spirit.

Jesus wanted to speak in terms we would understand, and so He used the familiar ones of "parent and child." Jesus always calls Himself the Son, the Son begotten of the Father,

in an eternal begetting, which has no beginning or end.
Begetting expresses a relationship, an activity which simply is.
Jesus is the result of a fecundity, a fecundity of love. Fr Finet
called God the Son the "given love."

How do we get close to all this? The Father is the source;
He is alone in the act of begetting. This thought must be
purified: this isn't fatherhood distinct from motherhood; it
includes both. He is Father all alone. His begetting never
began and will never cease—it is the essence of God as
Father. So the Father is only Father. The essence of God is
love. St Thomas described God as the "prime" or "unmoved"
mover, the cause of all things. This is a very significant idea if
we meditate on it.

The Holy Spirit

The Holy Spirit is the activity within God known as
"procession." The Father doesn't proceed from any other
divine person, while the Son is begotten of the Father. The
Spirit proceeds from the Father and the Son. The real mystery
is that one person of these three is not superior to the others.
The Holy Spirit lives in our depths and sanctifies us. The gift
of the Spirit is one of the Church's gifts to help us
understand—He gives us balance in our lives: "What the soul
is to the human body, the Holy Spirit is to the Body of Christ,
which is the Church." (CCC 797)

Love is an outpouring of self to the one we love. We
receive love from the ones who love us. Love is shared
between the persons of the Trinity. We usually speak of the
spirit of love as coming from the Holy Spirit. The marvellous
fact is that each of these three persons possesses the totality of
the divinity in themselves. This is celebrated in the "Te
Deum." God is Father, Son and Spirit; three persons but one
God: this is the mystery—we can state it but not explain it.

Jesus spoke of the work of the Holy Spirit at the Last
Supper:

These things I have spoken to you, while I am still with you. But the Counselor, the Holy Spirit, whom the Father will send in my name, he will teach you all things, and bring to your remembrance all that I have said to you. (John 14:25-26) But when the Counselor comes, whom I shall send to you from the Father, even the Spirit of truth, who proceeds from the Father, he will bear witness to me; and you also are witnesses, because you have been with me from the beginning. (John 15:26-27)

But now I am going to him who sent me; yet none of you asks me, "Where are you going?" But because I have said these things to you, sorrow has filled your hearts. Nevertheless I tell you the truth: it is to your advantage that I go away, for if I do not go away, the Counselor will not come to you; but if I go, I will send him to you. And when he comes, he will convince the world concerning sin and righteousness and judgment: concerning sin, because they do not believe in me; concerning righteousness, because I go to the Father, and you will see me no more; concerning judgment, because the ruler of this world is judged.

I have yet many things to say to you, but you cannot bear them now. When the Spirit of truth comes, he will guide you into all the truth; for he will not speak on his own authority, but whatever he hears he will speak, and he will declare to you the things that are to come. He will glorify me, for he will take what is mine and declare it to you. All that the Father has is mine; therefore I said that he will take what is mine and declare it to you. (John 16:5-15)

The Holy Spirit is much greater than anything we can actually feel of His actions in our soul. He is joined to our spirit just as He was to Jesus' human spirit. We are stimulated by the Holy Spirit to discover our own vocation, which includes adoring the Father and bringing other people likewise to adoration. Through prayer the Father gives us His Son, Jesus; the Holy Spirit helps us in our struggles and to realize that we really are being transformed into an image of the Son. This experience of the presence of the Holy Spirit within should be a continual one, where we see Him as a real person working in us. The Spirit is always given for a good purpose, even to sinners like us, in order to build up the community.

St Paul describes the meaning of prayer and the gifts of the Spirit in the context of the communion of the Saints:

> Therefore I want you to understand that no one speaking by the Spirit of God ever says "Jesus be cursed!" and no one can say "Jesus is Lord" except by the Holy Spirit. Now there are varieties of gifts, but the same Spirit; and there are varieties of service, but the same Lord; and there are varieties of working, but it is the same God who inspires them all in every one. To each is given the manifestation of the Spirit for the common good. (1 Cor 12:3-7)

St Paul also expressed the role of the Spirit in the hearts of the baptised in Chapter 8 of his letter to the Romans, in making them concerned with spiritual matters. We are not always able to grasp what He said. The person who doesn't pray is influenced more by the effects of original sin; they live according to the flesh, and can't please God. If our mind is on spiritual matters then we can have peace and life. If the Spirit of God dwells in us, Christ is in us and we are truly alive. This is our great hope. Those led by the Spirit are sons of God, and the same Spirit enables them to say, "Our Father." When moved in this way we begin to act like sons of God.

Trinitarian Love

The Holy Trinity expresses the fact that God is love, He who gives and receives love. We enter into this mystery when we act in charity, when we "sing" the Trinity. Charity is the love of God which is given or received; if it is in our heart then we can have the dynamism of the Trinity. If we enter into intimate contemplation of Christ then we are getting right to the heart of the Trinity. Even so, the whole of the divine substance is found in Jesus. The grace of the Trinity pours forth through the heart of Mary; she received the Son in His fullness. For human couples, begetting is not the whole of their existence. So the words used are similar, but have different meanings. We have to think again about human paternity. It is associated, in some ways, with authority and this includes calling priests "Father." St Paul spoke of begetting his spiritual children, while Marthe's constant prayer was a lifting up of her heart, through Mary, to the Trinity, as in the following:

> Beloved Mother, you who know so well the paths of holiness and love; teach us to lift up our mind and heart often to God, to fix our respectful and loving attention on the Trinity. And since you walk with us on the path of eternal life, do not remain a stranger to the weak pilgrims your charity is ready to welcome. Turn your merciful face to us. Draw us into your light. Flood us with your kindnesses. Take us into the light and the love. Always take us further and higher into the splendours of heaven. Let nothing ever trouble our peace, nor turn us from the thought of God. But let each minute take us further into the depths of the awesome mystery, till the day when our soul—fully receptive to the light of divine union—will see all things in eternal love and unity. Amen.

It is remarkable that Marthe could write like this; but she wrote under the influence of grace, of extraordinary gifts which are not given to many. This was a sign of God's special love for her; she was someone who had a special devotion to Our Lady, following St Louis de Montfort. Marthe's Cause for beatification is proceeding, and her writings have the quality of a Doctor of the Church. It's often easier for simple people to understand her writings; she wrote so well and clearly under this special grace.

10

The Blessed Virgin Mary
Our Spiritual Mother

What the Catholic faith believes about Mary is based on what it believes about Christ, and what it teaches about Mary illumines in turn its faith in Christ. (CCC 487)

God proved His love for us by giving us His mother—Mary. God goes through the Blessed Virgin; she lived by faith, the true way to God. We need to pray through Mary—then our prayer will be full of tenderness. The Blessed Virgin was there in the Gospels with a hidden but very important presence. She was present at the most important moments of Jesus' life: at His birth in Bethlehem, at the start of His public ministry at Cana, and at the foot of the Cross to offer Him up to His Eternal Father.

Mary, the all-holy ever-virgin Mother of God, is the masterwork of the mission of the Son and the Spirit in the fullness of time. For the first time in the plan of salvation and because his Spirit had prepared her, the Father found the dwelling place where his Son and his Spirit could dwell among men. In this sense the Church's Tradition has often read the most beautiful texts on wisdom in relation to Mary. Mary is acclaimed and represented in the liturgy as the "Seat of Wisdom." In her, the "wonders of God" that the Spirit was to fulfill in Christ and the Church began to be manifested ... (CCC 721)

The Annunciation

In the sixth month the angel Gabriel was sent from God to a city of Galilee named Nazareth, to a virgin betrothed to a man whose name was Joseph, of the house of David; and the virgin's name was Mary. And he came to her and said, "Hail, full of grace, the Lord is with you!" But she was greatly troubled at the saying, and considered in her mind what sort of greeting this might be. And the angel said to her, "Do not be afraid, Mary, for you have found favor with God. And behold, you will conceive in your womb and bear a son, and you shall call his name Jesus. He will be great, and will be called the Son of the Most High; and the Lord God will give to him the throne of his father David, and he will reign over the house of Jacob for ever; and of his kingdom there will be no end."

And Mary said to the angel, "How shall this be, since I have no husband?" And the angel said to her, "The Holy Spirit will come upon you, and the power of the Most High will overshadow you; therefore the child to be born will be called holy, the Son of God. And behold, your kinswoman Elizabeth in her old age has also conceived a son; and this is the sixth month with her who was called barren. For with God nothing will be impossible." And Mary said, "Behold, I am the handmaid of the Lord; let it be to me according to your word." And the angel departed from her. (Luke 1:26-38)

St Luke was a first generation Christian and a companion of St Paul; he could only have gained this information from Our Lady herself. This passage sees Mary as a young girl, a virgin, who sees the Angel Gabriel who has been sent to her; he finds her "full of Grace," pure and radically resplendent. Mary was free from all stain of sin and the angel felt the presence of God within her; she was intelligent and fully aware of the importance of what was happening to her. She was momentarily disturbed by the angel's greeting but her desire made her open to God. Mary probably used the women of the Old Testament as role models; at least she must have read about them in the Scriptures. However, she knew much more about the real meaning of the Scriptures than the Jews who were also waiting for the Messiah. The Annunciation was for Mary the time when she became fully aware of who she was and her mission.

The great sin of human beings is laziness, becoming fed up, and not bothering about life. The greatness and misery of Man is shown in this; God's grace gives us liberty and Mary could have refused her role. So she must have had an extraordinary gift of the Holy Spirit to enable her to understand her place in the mystery of salvation, and accept it in faith.

The angel explained that she would become a Mother, giving birth and educating her child. Mary wondered how as a virgin she could conceive; she wasn't looking for proof but an explanation. Mary didn't doubt God's power and didn't hesitate: she accepted her role as God's servant, giving back her gifts of purity, will, and intelligence. Faith can move mountains: it is capable of great things. Mary's great faith tells us why she was suitable to be chosen from the whole human race to be the Mother of God.

We too need to become aware of our role, what God expects of us. It can be a struggle to live the Christian life, and we need to keep the finite nature of the world in mind. We have to be purified and take refuge near Mary; we all have a mission in the world. We are all wounded in some way and so need Mary's help, but paradoxically, the weakest of children can often be closest to God. We need Mary's tenderness; she prays, desires, searches and asks for us. She, too, was unsure of what God wanted and sought clarification. Despite the fact that she was only a young girl, she still fulfilled her role of crushing the head of the devil.

Mary was extraordinarily ordinary; people thought of the Holy family as normal, so we need to really know them to understand their exceptional nature. Mary didn't go into ecstasy at the angel's words. Her generosity and humility kept her feet on the ground. The Spirit spoke to Mary and told her that God would do the impossible, but she was also called to play her part. Mary was betrothed to St Joseph and saw him as the one chosen by God for her.

Mary lived an ordinary life—this was Marthe's firm position. God wanted to embrace man's situation fully and so he took the last place in poverty and humility. Mary lived a life of faith, conscious of God's presence and love. The Holy Spirit gave Mary the trust to say "Yes."

The Birth of Jesus

In those days a decree went out from Caesar Augustus that all the world should be enrolled. This was the first enrollment, when Quirinius was governor of Syria. And all went to be enrolled, each to his own city. And Joseph also went up from Galilee, from the city of Nazareth, to Judea, to the city of David, which is called Bethlehem, because he was of the house and lineage of David, to be enrolled with Mary, his betrothed, who was with child. And while they were there, the time came for her to be delivered. And she gave birth to her first-born son and wrapped him in swaddling cloths, and laid him in a manger, because there was no place for them in the inn. And in that region there were shepherds out in the field, keeping watch over their flock by night.

And an angel of the Lord appeared to them, and the glory of the Lord shone around them, and they were filled with fear. And the angel said to them, "Be not afraid; for behold, I bring you good news of a great joy which will come to all the people; for to you is born this day in the city of David a Savior, who is Christ the Lord. And this will be a sign for you: you will find a babe wrapped in swaddling cloths and lying in a manger." And suddenly there was with the angel a multitude of the heavenly host praising God and saying, "Glory to God in the highest, and on earth peace among men with whom he is pleased!"

When the angels went away from them into heaven, the shepherds said to one another, "Let us go over to Bethlehem and see this thing that has happened, which the Lord has made known to us." And they went with haste, and found Mary and

Joseph, and the babe lying in a manger. And when they saw it they made known the saying which had been told them concerning this child; and all who heard it wondered at what the shepherds told them. But Mary kept all these things, pondering them in her heart. And the shepherds returned, glorifying and praising God for all they had heard and seen, as it had been told them. (Luke 2:1-20)

After the betrothal of Joseph and Mary they had to go to Bethlehem to be inscribed and pay their taxes to Rome. The child was born in a stable as an inn wasn't a suitable place for a woman about to give birth. Mary conceived and gave birth as a virgin—this is a mystery proclaimed by the Church in which God's transcendent action is manifested. The birth of Jesus contains elements of both the transfiguration and the resurrection. The mystery of Jesus' birth is symbolic of the way He did everything, in humility and without fuss or noise. Jesus was the first born, spiritually, of all men, so Mary is the spiritual mother of all men.

We need to be aware of the role of the Church's tradition in safeguarding all this. The shepherds were humble and poor, but joyous. They saw the baby Jesus as their Savior, Messiah, and Lord. Jesus is the "Word" who is silent at birth, and starts His life in silence. When people are humble they are like children and so, Christ-like. This is something which is difficult for sophisticated adults to grasp.

Mary's Role in the Church

God wished to use Mary to become incarnate. Christ is the only Mediator between God and man: how we do explain this tension as regards Mary's role as mediatrix? Mary was honored by God but she also had much confidence put in her—as the Magnificat foretold, all generations have indeed called her blessed. Through the centuries, many of the saints such as St Bernard and St Louis de Montfort have emphasized her very important position in the life of the Church:

Mary's role in the Church is inseparable from her union with Christ and flows directly from it. ... By her complete adherence to the Father's will, to his Son's redemptive work, and to every prompting of the Holy Spirit, the Virgin Mary is the Church's model of faith and charity. Thus she is a 'preeminent and . . . wholly unique member of the Church'; indeed, she is the 'exemplary realization' (typus) of the Church. (CCC 964, 967)

God loves man so much that He wanted to honor man; He became man by a woman, Mary. This mediation of Mary's is unique; she was specially chosen by God from her Immaculate Conception. There is a harmony and unity in the will of God. The cult of Mary gives Man a new importance since she was used by God in such an important way. Mary in her fecund virginity rehumanised life—she radically and fundamentally gave us back a true sense of dignity.

In the history of the Church, when Mary has been in her rightful position, then its work has flourished. Mary is the faithful one whose fidelity was her finest prayer. We should be faithful in all we do; this is the best prayer. Everyone who is to become a son of God needs a mother—God wished it to be that way. Mary was not the "transit camp" of redemption; redemption was dependent on her will and cooperation. She said "yes" and the Word was made flesh. This indicates an unheard of faith. We fell into sin by the "no" of our first parents. The "yes" of Christ, a divine person, saves us. God willed this and so chose Mary. She said her "yes" at the beginning of Jesus' public life and finally at the foot of the Cross—she was fully a part of what happened. Her place in the role of redemption is seen at key points of the Gospel.

Mary is intimately a part of the theology of the Church. Writers such as St John the Evangelist and Polycarp, an early martyr, speak of her role, and the tradition of the Immaculate Conception goes back to the early centuries. Jesus was the only person ever to choose His mother, and Mary was Queen in the sense that Jesus was obedient to her and Joseph. Mary was full of glory at her death—full of all that God could wish for in creation. She merited it by her co-operation in Christ's sufferings: God wanted her to merit the privilege of her Assumption. Mary was immaculate but lived in mercy and contrition, despite the fact that she was sinless; she had the life of the Trinity flowing in her soul. Mary was pure and holy, full of grace; she prays for us sinners. The Virgin Mary is near us as the perfect Woman, full of dignity, who knows us as her spiritual children better than anyone: she wants us to become other Christs. Mary has been given the power to raise us up in this way.

Marthe said that Mary was the Mother of the Foyers, and likewise emphasised her role in making us like her son Jesus. So we need to remember she is there and will lead us to the heart of everything; but we have to daily renew our choice of her as Mother and Queen. Mary is the most beautiful creature God has created—she is a better model and help for us than the angels. Mary is the summit of creation in a human being.

Jesus wanted to be a real man and so He made a true desire grow in the heart of His mother, Mary. God heard her prayers since she was perfectly aware and responsible, but also truly humble. God used the weakness of a woman, but Mary was also harmonious and sinless. Adam was the prototype of Jesus as Eve was of Mary; our redemption means we must see everything through Christ. So humanism for the Christian is Christ, who had to carry out His combat by means of the will and in doing so conquered death.

The people who were converted at the time of Pentecost asked the Apostles, "What must we do?" Their conversion demanded a complete change of mind and heart. When we are close to Mary she guides us, and not just in the sense of our intelligence but of everything which exists, giving us access to her total understanding.

11

The Church in the World

The mission of Christ and the Holy Spirit is brought to completion in the Church, which is the Body of Christ and the Temple of the Holy Spirit. This joint mission henceforth brings Christ's faithful to share in his communion with the Father in the Holy Spirit. ... Thus the Church's mission is not an addition to that of Christ and the Holy Spirit, but is its sacrament: in her whole being and in all her members, the Church is sent to announce, bear witness, make present, and spread the mystery of the communion of the Holy Trinity. (CCC 737-38)

The pardon and love of the Church are proofs of its divine origin. God chose us to fulfill a great plan, building up the body of which His Son is the head. We need to love our parents to understand their intuitions and ways of doing things. Similarly we need to love the Church to understand her "family" traditions; these are important and shouldn't be neglected.

The basic Constitution of the Church was defined more fully during the Second Vatican Council. Before this, the approach had been more dogmatic. The Council defined how the Church should be and see itself—*Lumen Gentium*—The Light of the World. This outlines how the mystery of the Church in the world has a rhythm of its own; it is essentially different from other communities. The great mystery of the Church, in whatever part of the world it is found, is the mystery of the Trinity; this denotes the essential nature of the

Church. We enter into the life of the Trinity through the Church; this wasn't a prominent idea in older forms of catechesis. The Church is the mystery of the life of the Trinity; so we are also called to live this Trinitarian life. How do we do this in practise? We need to reflect on the above to understand and interiorize these ideas.

Lumen Gentium next discusses the role of the hierarchy, then the laity, eschatology, and finally in the last chapter, Mary. The Fathers of the Council wanted a special constitution for Mary, but this might have isolated her and so finally she was put in her proper place—inside the mystery of the Church. She was the first member of the Church and lived the full life of the Trinity. She is the distributor of grace and the Mother of divine grace. There is no real Church without Mary—she is essential to its nature.

St Paul and the Church

The foundation for the Church's view of itself is found in the letter of St Paul to the Ephesians, which describes the Mystery of Salvation and of the Church. We have already looked at this passage above, in the context of looking at the person of Christ, but it is also applicable to the Church, the Bride of Christ.

> Blessed be the God and Father of our Lord Jesus Christ, who has blessed us in Christ with every spiritual blessing in the heavenly places, even as he chose us in him before the foundation of the world, that we should be holy and blameless before him. He destined us in love to be his sons through Jesus Christ, according to the purpose of his will, to the praise of his glorious grace which he freely bestowed on us in the Beloved. In him we have redemption through his blood, the forgiveness of our trespasses, according to the riches of his grace which he lavished upon us.
>
> For he has made known to us in all wisdom and insight the mystery of his will, according to his purpose which he set forth in Christ as a plan for the fulness of time, to unite all things in him, things in heaven and things on earth. In him, according to

the purpose of him who accomplishes all things according to the counsel of his will, we who first hoped in Christ have been destined and appointed to live for the praise of his glory. In him you also, who have heard the word of truth, the gospel of your salvation, and have believed in him, were sealed with the promised Holy Spirit, which is the guarantee of our inheritance until we acquire possession of it, to the praise of his glory. (Eph 1:3-14)

This first chapter is recited in the Office, the offical prayer of the Church, which is said by priests and religious. It speaks of the Father, Son and Spirit and is a hymn of joy. God blesses us and fills us with His blessings; it echoes the triple amen in the doxology of the Mass. We are joined to the angels and archangels and have our freedom through Christ's death. Those who suffer in the Church—and all are included—share in the saving activity of Christ. The offering of an individual's suffering with Christ has great value: the Church needs it.

The Church Today

The Second Vatican Council has explained and put into order many things in the life of the Church. The externals of the Church aren't the same as the Church itself. We can't talk about the presence of the Church without looking at the Scriptures—other writings are secondary in this respect. There have been different historical aspects in other councils, such as Trent. In the early history of the Church there was more of an emphasis on apologetics; there were many attacks which had to be resisted. Church beliefs were clarified in the early Councils. So in this sense, Vatican II is the Church's reply to the long term problems caused by the Reformation.

Luther is an example of what happens when trust in God, and the Church, goes, and we start analyzing with reason alone—problems arise. We have a different view of the Pope today—the old temporal power has gone. Modern Popes have had to live with many contradictions but we have been blessed with a series of holy and even extraordinary men, particularly in the case of John Paul II, who in his writings showed himself to be sensitive to all the problems of the world. The teachings of the Popes are misinterpreted by people who only look at the surface and not the interior. The Pope is the sign of the unity of the Episcopal college, rather in the way that the spokes of a bicycle are connected to the hub; he is a sign of visible unity.

Ecumenism begins with looking at the nature of the Church and not with such matters as the role of the Pope. We need to pray for our brother Orthodox Christians, for unity, and also for those Catholics and others who suffered persecution under communism. The good of Jesus Christ is the basis of our belief and of ecumenism—we look to the Father who has been revealed by Christ.

The Church needs to be militant and have strength and direction—we should think more about the conversion of souls. We have to fight our own inner selfishness and the spirit of the world. We need to recognise our own weakness and work hard to be faithful. All sorts of people are needed in the Church today, since the European temperament, whether Latin or Northern can be too limited—we need to discover the spiritual freedom of African, Asian, and Latin American Christians. As the early Jesuit missionaries discovered, these peoples live the reality of God in another way, but it is the same Jesus who needs to be discovered by all.

Baptism

Baptism is the sacrament by which we become a part of the Church.

> Now when all the people were baptized, and when Jesus also had been baptized and was praying, the heaven was opened, and the Holy Spirit descended upon him in bodily form, as a dove, and a voice came from heaven, "Thou art my beloved Son; with thee I am well pleased." (Luke 3:21-22)

We see how the Heart of Jesus was affected by the Spirit in this wonderful passage; this is a text we need to look at carefully. John the Baptist had previously spoken of how the Messiah would deal with all those things which were offensive to God, and now Jesus had entered on the scene. He was praying after His own Baptism, and the Baptist saw the Spirit descending on Him like a dove; the Spirit also descends on us when we are baptised, as we assume the faith of our parents. But now we have to realize this for ourselves and renew our Baptismal promises. The Holy Spirit can then illuminate our hearts:

> Baptism, the original and full sign of which is immersion, efficaciously signifies the descent into the tomb by the Christian who dies to sin with Christ in order to live a new life. 'We were buried therefore with him by baptism into death, so that as Christ was raised from the dead by the glory of the Father, we too might walk in newness of life.' (CCC 628)

We have not kept our Baptismal promises, but when we realize that Jesus made himself a "slave" for our sakes, being obedient to His death on the Cross, we can see the need to understand ourselves as true children of God, as part of the body of Christ. We can lose this status through our sins, or by failing to live up to our Baptismal promises. We can merit anger and rejection and so we shouldn't seek to come by ourselves before God, rather, we need someone to act for us, a mediator. So we go to the Father through Jesus and Mary. We have all passed through water, spirit and blood; Baptism, confirmation, and our redemption. Baptism imprints a "character" on our souls, an indelible mark which cannot be taken away by sin.

Nowadays, Man doesn't realize he has a capacity for eternity within him. We must strengthen this reality in us through the sacraments and not just see them as rituals. The power of the sacraments is not due to the holiness of the Priest:

From the moment that a sacrament is celebrated in accordance with the intention of the Church, the power of Christ and His Spirit acts in and through it, independently of the personal holiness of the minister. Nevertheless, the fruits of the sacraments also depend on the disposition of the one who receives them. (CCC 1128)

How does Baptism wipe out original sin?—this is a lack of sanctifying grace, and Baptism removes this defect and allows us to become "divinized" through the sacrament: "By Baptism all sins are forgiven, original sin and all personal sins, as well as all punishment for sin. (CCC 1263)"

Our Lady lived the interior disposition of one who wasn't affected by original sin—the mark of the Trinity was fully within her; we too have this mark when we are baptised and the grace of Jesus is given to us. So we must develop our life with God and see the day of our Baptism as a very important one. Baptism has an extraordinary greatness—if we can understand this, then our love for God can grow greater, and we can better appreciate this gift given us by Jesus.

12

The Sacraments of Confession & Anointing

We must go to Confession regularly and seek out a spiritual director; it is the sacrament of God's care. We need to be reconciled with God regularly in the Sacrament of Confession, to purify ourselves to worthily adore Him. We are all sinners who don't take God seriously enough. The return of the "prodigal" son is the pattern for many people's lives— but we can also ask pardon for others through the power of the mystical body which links us all. We need to discover that God is our Father. He wants to open our hearts to discover what is evil, but more importantly to His presence and tenderness—this is the reason for our being.

Thus, it is important to have a developed understanding of conscience—not to overlook things but equally not to overdo things and become scrupulous. We have to deal with all these matters of conscience with delicacy and generosity. Even so, it is vitally important that we recognize our sinfulness and take it seriously—daily purification from sin is important for us— St Paul was angry with people who didn't receive Holy Communion with the right dispositions. We should have the sort of attitude that enables us to admit we have made a mistake, even to a little child—we must have this humility.

We must confess our poverty of spirit and look into the dark corners of our soul. The Holy Spirit invites us to go further and experience the joy of forgiveness:

> The confession (or disclosure) of sins, even from a simply human point of view, frees us and facilitates our reconciliation with others. Through such an admission man looks squarely at the sins he is guilty of, takes responsibility for them, and thereby opens himself again to God and to the communion of the Church in order to make a new future possible. (CCC 1455)

In the measure that we discover the weakness of our being, we discover the greatness and power of the mercy of God. So we have to be people who combat sin with faith, hope, and love. Our interior fight is against sensuality. God is waiting for us in Confession, the sacrament of His tenderness. We must be aware of our own weaknesses and failings, our weakened powers and faculties. Don't imagine that you can't fall: we are all fragile and vacillating. We have to be constantly aware of this and not just depend on rules and regulations, or routines. There is thus a fundamental need for humility. Jesus is constantly restoring life to us spiritually and opening for us a unique aspect of fraternal charity.

We should make an act of contrition if we find ourselves falling away. It is humiliating to keep coming back to the same sins in Confession—but it is very necessary. Confession is a great grace, a gift, a turning of the heart to God. We are seeking the tenderness of God and need to make an act of confidence in Him. Going to Confession is a sign that we are on the right road. We should see the Sacrament of Penance as a wellspring in our life, and realise that the divine life in us depends very much on the extent to which we recognise our own faults and work to minimise them. We must also have contrition for our sins, since we need to be in a state of repentance to pray properly. Confession has the power of conversion—but we shouldn't put it off for too long. The

Holy Spirit leads us to ask for pardon and forgiveness. Grace comes to us through our cross and our own prayer.

This grace leads to a substantial change in our souls, one which brings enlightenment. If we fight our temptations then repentance becomes a habit, which is fulfilled in our reception of the Eucharist. We don't arrive at a state of "goodness" though; we always remain totally dependant on God. We can't wilfully abandon Confession, and should go whenever we need the sacrament. We need to prepare our hearts for Confession; we shouldn't be too enclosed. Lack of love towards God and others are the things we need to be considering. How do we do use our gifts, what are the things we could have done, our sins of omission? Regarding our lack of love towards God; how much time do we give to deepen our faith? In short, we need to accept our sinfulness and confess our sins.

The Forgiveness of Christ

There is a big difference between falling into sin as we are getting worse spiritually, that is becoming lukewarm, and falling as we are getting better and becoming more fervent. We need to look at the Lord continually, and not look at ourselves too much. This means not being too scrupulous, which is a sign of pride. God allows our sin and weakness but is pleased to see our sorrow for our sins. The mirror which we look at is God Himself, Jesus Christ. His mercy is infinite for those who reverence and fear Him. This attitude of humility makes us more childlike and filial, more contrite and thankful. We must be aware of becoming lukewarm; our contrition is the most beautiful act of love we can make. St Augustine emphasised the mercy of God in his *Confessions*. We remain sinners even when forgiven; but we also become holy, alive, and agreeable to God. Marthe felt sin very acutely: we have mostly lost this sense of sin. Confession is a sacrament which can't be replaced.

Parishioners should help their Priest, but without flattery! They should be audacious and ask for Confession if necessary. This process of drawing out the Fatherhood from the heart of the Priest is very beneficial since they often feel their solitude in a crushing way.

We must take time to contemplate the way in which our sins have been forgiven through Christ's sacrifice of blood; we gain our freedom this way. Luther spoke of the blood of Christ covering us—but this is incorrect—it actually purifies us from within. Grace is the mercy of God. This pardoning of sins is continued in the Eucharist as sacrifice. Grace without limit flows over us. This eternal rhythm transcends nature; such is the richness of grace.

Parables of Forgiveness

St Luke described three of Jesus' parables which tell of God's mercy, those of the lost sheep, the lost drachma, and the lost or "prodigal" son. Each of the parables involves a search which symbolises the Father's search for us, as He comes to forgive us our sins.

> Now the tax collectors and sinners were all drawing near to hear him. And the Pharisees and the scribes murmured, saying, "This man receives sinners and eats with them." So he told them this parable: "What man of you, having a hundred sheep, if he has lost one of them, does not leave the ninety-nine in the wilderness, and go after the one which is lost, until he finds it? And when he has found it, he lays it on his shoulders, rejoicing. And when he comes home, he calls together his friends and his neighbors, saying to them, 'Rejoice with me, for I have found my sheep which was lost.'
>
> Just so, I tell you, there will be more joy in heaven over one sinner who repents than over ninety-nine righteous persons who need no repentance.
>
> Or what woman, having ten silver coins, if she loses one coin, does not light a lamp and sweep the house and seek diligently until she finds it? And when she has found it, she calls

together her friends and neighbors, saying, 'Rejoice with me, for I have found the coin which I had lost.' Just so, I tell you, there is joy before the angels of God over one sinner who repents." (Luke 15:1-10).

Jesus' human heart was concerned for every lost person; He searches continually to find us with God's infinite love. We need to be aware of the destructive effects of sin on ourselves and on the Body of Christ, which is the Church—a lost person means it isn't complete. Jesus is full of joy at the return of the sinner; "respectable" people may be a bit like the Pharisees in this context. Mary had an acute perception of sin—so we ask her to pray for us sinners. Jesus is the eternal, untiring, shepherd. We should leave our troubles on one side, waiting for the Father and listening to Him. Thus, we need to go very often to receive God's mercy in Confession; but we must avoid making it just something mechanical.

The story of the "prodigal" son, which we considered above in the context of understanding ourselves as children of God, is very important if we are to understand the full significance of the Sacrament of Confession. The fall of the son gives the devil a degree of power over him. He asks for his inheritance; this is a reflection of the sin of Adam and his desire to be independent of God. Nothing is really due to us or ours by right. But God respects our decisions even if they are sinful; he knew that some people would reject eternal life. All our acts have their origin in God: even so, it is difficult for us to understand why God allows sin—it is a mystery to us.

The son squandered his inheritance and rejected his father's love. Often, we become too wrapped up in ourselves, and it then becomes difficult to be faithful. We have to concentrate and not become dissipated. When the son realises he is dying of hunger he decides to go home. He needed solitude and deprivation to realise his need for his father. He confesses his faults but this is imperfect contrition since he is doing it because he is hungry. So the son returns, although the father sees him first and was waiting for him all the time. This causes the older son to become angry; he doesn't think of the father's mercy; he is probably waiting for his father to die so he can have all the inheritance. The father clasps his lost son tenderly and calls for a celebration, a sign of the new covenant and the Eucharistic meal. How will he convert the older son who is so avaricious? He calls his younger brother "this son of yours," whereas the father gently reproves him by calling him "your brother." A vital necessity in life is to celebrate and rejoice at times—especially when people return to God. We need to become aware of the tenderness of God and see how we can show this to others so they are converted. Only God, though, can really accomplish this change of heart.

The Sacrament of the Sick

> By the sacred anointing of the sick and the prayer of the priests the whole Church commends those who are ill to the suffering and glorified Lord, that he may raise them up and save them. And indeed she exhorts them to contribute to the good of the People of God by freely uniting themselves to the Passion and death of Christ. (CCC 1499)

St James said that if someone was ill, the Priest should be called and the person anointed: "Is any among you sick? Let him call for the elders of the church, and let them pray over him, anointing him with oil in the name of the Lord, and the prayer of faith will save the sick man, and the Lord will raise him up; and if he has committed sins, he will be forgiven." (James 5:14-15)

This sacrament isn't just for the dying—it's also for the sick or even for aged persons; it is a remedy for sicknesses of body and soul. It shouldn't be neglected as a means of wholeness, as has tended to happen in the past. We shouldn't wait until an illness is too serious; it may then be too late for the sacrament to have its full effect. This sacrament is also necessary, on occasion, for children. The role of the Sacrament of the sick is underrated. Jesus cured the sick and when this sacrament is used in conjunction with medical science it can mean extra time for people to prepare for death. The grace of the sacrament can also include an understanding for the sick person that they won't get well, that perhaps suffering is their vocation. However, good health does help us to praise God.

13

The Mass, Holy Communion,
& the Priesthood

We must make room in our day for prayer, and if possible, the Mass. Our lives should be centred on the Eucharist, which is the tenderness of Jesus expressing the tenderness of the Father. Jesus' love for his people is expressed in the mystery of the Eucharist: which is,

> the source and summit of the Christian life. The other sacraments, and indeed all ecclesiastical ministries and works of the apostolate, are bound up with the Eucharist and are oriented toward it. For in the blessed Eucharist is contained the whole spiritual good of the Church, namely Christ himself, our Pasch. (CCC 1324)

We shouldn't be afraid to enter into the Heart of Jesus and see the Eucharist as a festival celebrating God's intervention for His people. It is a liturgy of reconciliation and redemption. The old festival of the Jewish Passover was superseded by a new one with a new Passover lamb, Jesus, offered to the Father for us. This festival is fulfilled in the Mass. As the *Catechism* states: "The whole liturgical life of the Church revolves around the Eucharistic sacrifice and the sacraments." (1113)

We need to get to the depths of the Mass, which is the same sacrifice throughout the world. The liturgy of the Mass puts us in touch with the Heart of Jesus, with His enthusiasm and love. In our effort to pray we begin to understand this. We need to help children to enter into the mystery of the Mass; perhaps slowing down a bit and explaining things to them more fully. We need to leave them free but also provoke them to think more deeply about their faith. If we do what is possible, then God will do the impossible. Jesus purifies us, He sanctifies us, and offers us to the Father in the great offering of the Mass.

In reading the Gospels we need to look closely at the person of Jesus; this is the correct way to approach the Scriptures. We should make this an interior process and ask ourselves what Jesus' gestures really mean. We shouldn't get tired of reading the Scriptures, realising that it is the creator God who is doing the things we read about.

At the Last Supper Jesus knew it was His hour to leave the world and go to His Father. He knew how this would happen and how He would have to experience the ultimate in obedience to the Father's will, and in this way fulfil His mission. He knew He would have to suffer arrest, condemnation, scourging, the carrying of the Cross, the crowning with thorns, and His Crucifixion. He knew He would have to experience all that.

We can fear suffering, so how must Jesus have felt with His inner knowledge as God? He was without sin and was going to the Father, but was also one with us. He was consubstantial with the father, and yet felt the full revolt of all the sins of mankind. We need to lean, like the apostle John, on the Heart of Jesus, so we can be of help to our brothers, doing what we can for them. Our mission of co-redemption involves this. Marthe suffered and offered herself to God for the sins of the world. Why are we so selfish and egoistic? All this seems like madness to the world, but we do have a real solidarity with all who are suffering.

Thus, Jesus knew all this had been put into His hands. He had the honour from His Father of suffering for the sake of mankind. Marthe, too, offered all for her fellow men and women, her legs, her eyes—she became blind—her whole being. The Eucharist is the basis of the Christian life, and Marthe was fed and nourished entirely by Holy Communion. We need to understand Jesus' thoughts and feelings on Maundy Thursday to really understand the Eucharist. The essential point of the following text is that it is Eucharistic.

The Washing of the Disciples' feet

And during supper, when the devil had already put it into the heart of Judas Iscariot, Simon's son, to betray him, Jesus, knowing that the Father had given all things into his hands, and that he had come from God and was going to God, rose from supper, laid aside his garments, and girded himself with a towel. (John 13:2-4)

Jesus knew it was time to return to the Father. There is a mixture of the ordinary and the sublime in the text; St John is the most precise of the Gospel writers. He describes the practical details and shows us the spiritual through everyday things. We must dig deep in our meditations.

Then he poured water into a basin, and began to wash the disciples' feet, and to wipe them with the towel with which he was girded. He came to Simon Peter; and Peter said to him, "Lord, do you wash my feet?" Jesus answered him, "What I am doing you do not know now, but afterward you will understand." Peter said to him, "You shall never wash my feet." Jesus answered him, "If I do not wash you, you have no part in me." Simon Peter said to him, "Lord, not my feet only but also my hands and my head!" Jesus said to him, "He who has bathed does not need to wash, except for his feet, but he is clean all over; and you are clean, but not every one of you." For he knew who was to betray him; that was why he said, "You are not all clean." (John 13:5-11)

Unless Peter allows his feet to be washed he won't be a part of Jesus' thinking, His way of life and commission. St John was writing as an old man with a fatherly love for his community. He was christianizing the hearts of his people. John's charism involved teaching and contemplation.

> When he had washed their feet, and taken his garments, and resumed his place, he said to them, "Do you know what I have done to you? You call me Teacher and Lord; and you are right, for so I am. If I then, your Lord and Teacher, have washed your feet, you also ought to wash one another's feet. For I have given you an example, that you also should do as I have done to you. Truly, truly, I say to you, a servant is not greater than his master; nor is he who is sent greater than he who sent him. If you know these things, blessed are you if you do them. (John 13:12-17)

Jesus got up from the table to start to wash His disciples' feet: His were ordinary actions; taking up a towel, pouring water and wiping their feet. To give a service to others under the inspiration of the Holy Spirit, we need to go right to the end; it's often difficult for us to persevere, but this shows the sincerity of our heart to others. God's tenderness is expressed in Jesus' sufferings and His willingness to serve others. Jesus asked the disciples if they understood the significance of what He had done for them—not just the physical washing—but also the feelings and love behind the actions, which were done from the heart. The Holy Spirit will lead us to understand this if we are docile; but we need to have a willingness to learn.

The final point of this passage is the necessity of "doing" rather than observing. Do we really look after people? There is a contrast between the practical details and their sublime inner meaning. These are the actions of the Word of God and are seen as sacramental. They show how Jesus understood His mission. According to Marthe, Jesus' discourse at this time also concerned penance, confession, repentance and justification; her spiritual experiences when she experienced the Passion were later transcribed. The most important thing about the Gospel meditations produced by Marthe is to appreciate them as things close to the Heart of Jesus. Scripture always comes before writings such as those of Marthe, but these still have value.

Jesus in the Eucharist is present among us: "In the most blessed sacrament of the Eucharist 'the body and blood, together with the soul and divinity, of our Lord Jesus Christ and, therefore, the whole Christ is truly, really, and substantially contained.' " (CCC 1374)

The Eucharist is an echo of the multiplication of the loaves. Marthe stressed the importance of Mass—"Mass isn't an obligation, it's a necessity." Every soul is a victim; life is a Calvary for all of us. As St Paul said:

> I appeal to you therefore, brethren, by the mercies of God, to present your bodies as a living sacrifice, holy and acceptable to God, which is your spiritual worship. Do not be conformed to this world but be transformed by the renewal of your mind, that you may prove what is the will of God, what is good and acceptable and perfect. (Rom 12:1-2).

The body is an offering that we make to God, especially in the Mass where we offer up ourselves, all we have, all we do, to God. We need to recognize ourselves as sinners but make a sincere effort to be an offering without any leaven. So we confess our sins at the beginning of Mass as an act of purification. The Passover covenant brought the children of Israel out of Egypt. The new Passover of God sees Jesus as the bridegroom, with humanity as the bride. We eat the new Passover meal, the Eucharist, because we are not angels.

> And he took bread, and when he had given thanks he broke it and gave it to them, saying, 'This is my body which is given for you. Do this in remembrance of me.' And likewise the cup after supper, saying, 'This cup which is poured out for you is the new covenant in my blood.' (Luke 22:19-20)

In the middle of the meal Jesus gives us His flesh and blood! The simple and the sublime are together. We need to eat Jesus' flesh in order to have life in us. There is a great solemnity in the accounts of the institution of the Eucharist. Everything was foreseen including Peter's betrayal: presumption and discouragement are fundamental vices. Judas took a perverse pride in despair—he trusted in himself and didn't make an act of sorrow.

The Priesthood

Sacrifice implies the offering of something to someone, and in the religious sense requires a priesthood. There is also the "priesthood" we all have by virtue of our Baptism, by which we offer ourselves to God in the most fundamental way, but as the *Catechism* states: "The ordained ministry or ministerial priesthood is at the service of the Baptismal priesthood. The ordained priesthood guarantees that it really is Christ who acts in the sacraments through the Holy Spirit for the Church." (1120) Thus the ministerial priesthood is absolutely vital.

We offer ourselves to the extent that we are in solidarity with Christ; we offer ourselves and are offered to the Father. The Holy Spirit sharpens and builds our faith. This places the ministerial priesthood in its true context. It is Christ who chooses the Priest—this is not a democratic choice. God calls the individual to become a Priest and then sends him out; Holy Orders come from Christ. There will be no ministerial priesthood in heaven and Priests will be judged on their union with Christ. Priests are consecrated for the people of God. They pray for other people as well as themselves. The priesthood involves a life of service for others. A minister is one who serves. A Priest without people and vice versa is not a truly Christian community.

There is no Eucharist without the Priest so we need more Priests. Jesus said to pray for workers to the Lord of the harvest. We should pray for Priests, ask for what we want and need in the Church and do everything possible to promote this aim. The story of the widow and the unjust judge in the Gospel should be our model; she wore him down, and we, too, shouldn't cease to pray to God. Priestly vocations are difficult to nurture. Attractive seminaries are important with sound spiritual guidance. The priesthood cannot be replaced. We must pray and fast—more Priests are desperately needed. We shouldn't complain about people but pray! Each person has the responsibility to pray for more Priests.

The Priest is the minister or servant of the people; we should tell our priests what we want of them—they need feedback. Marthe dwelt on the idea of the Priest as "Father." Fatherhood implies one who understands, loves, suffers. It is up to us to draw this fatherhood out of our priests. We shouldn't upset our priests, but rather help them.

The Priest is greater than just his "person"; he is the only one who can say "This is my Body." There needs to be great mutual affection between Priest and people. Marthe adopted Fr Finet as her "spiritual Father"—she called him "mon Père"—"my Father." There is a greatness and poverty about a Priest, and it is up to the people to help them. The Priest is essentially a father who knows his children; there should be love and service between them. The fatherhood of the Priest comes from the Father in heaven. The Epistle to the Hebrews focuses on this principle of priesthood. The offering of the self which is implied in the priesthood of the baptised is what makes us a royal priesthood.

The letter to the Galatians has a sentence which shows the sort of attitude the Priest should have towards his people: "My little children, with whom I am again in travail until Christ be formed in you!" (Gal 4:19). This is the Priest's task—to form Christ in the hearts of the faithful. To offer Christ we need the Priest; but he must be a real Father and not just a "post-holder."

We need to pray for our Priests with Mary: we need Christ's presence through the Priest. He is God's intermediary for us; he isn't necessarily trying to teach us things we don't know but rather to lead us to know God in our hearts. The role of the preacher is that of a father guiding and helping his children. This is difficult as we find it hard to understand God's language, despite the fact that He is both tender and persistent—but He is also patient and prepared to wait for us.

14

Family Life, Marriage, & Society

Now the birth of Jesus Christ took place in this way. When his mother Mary had been betrothed to Joseph, before they came together she was found to be with child of the Holy Spirit; and her husband Joseph, being a just man and unwilling to put her to shame, resolved to divorce her quietly. But as he considered this, behold, an angel of the Lord appeared to him in a dream, saying, "Joseph, son of David, do not fear to take Mary your wife, for that which is conceived in her is of the Holy Spirit; she will bear a son, and you shall call his name Jesus, for he will save his people from their sins."

All this took place to fulfil what the Lord had spoken by the prophet: "Behold, a virgin shall conceive and bear a son, and his name shall be called Emmanuel" (which means, God with us). When Joseph woke from sleep, he did as the angel of the Lord commanded him; he took his wife, but knew her not until she had borne a son; and he called his name Jesus. (Matt 1:18-25)

We should note the tremendous graces received by Joseph, graces which gave him an affinity, in some respects, to the Immaculate Conception. Joseph was a just man, a man of honour. He had decided to divorce Mary informally. Joseph saw that a great mystery had passed in Mary's heart, and in his humility he felt unworthy to stay with her. Joseph wouldn't have thought of Mary as being pregnant outside marriage; he had too high an opinion of her. He realised her pregnancy must have come from God. Marthe described Joseph as the greatest human being after Mary. If we really love St Joseph we will have a true spirituality.

Joseph was going to send Mary away, but an angel appeared and told him what to do. There was a need for Mary to have a husband. Joseph understood that he was truly a father; all this points to the marvel of virginity within the Church. Mary and Joseph acted together spiritually; their marriage was spiritually consummated, their virginity was fruitful, and so Joseph was a true husband.

Parents and Children

We can ask for holiness for a child and it will be given. The gift of life is meant to build up the body of Christ. An unborn child can even be "educated" in the womb. Parents need to spend a lot of time with their children in order to truly love them; we should encourage their prayer as it is truly powerful.

Parents must love their children in order for them to grow. Children recognise if their parents really believe or not, if God is with them or not. Children and old people have a key role in the Church. It is a question of purity and innocence contrasted with age and experience, as well as suffering. We need to pray for people who can animate groups of children.

God gives us life through our parents, but they aren't its source or principle. We can learn how we really are by observing young children, in the way they are often very selfish. The world follows the evil and easy way, so there is a need for us to renew our spirit. Parents tend to want to bring out the intellectual qualities of their children, but this isn't necessarily God's way. A parent just can't warn a child against the tendency towards sin, there also has to be proper instruction, but it mustn't be overdone. Children often can't control their impulses, but despite this, they still need to have boundaries to their behaviour. We all have to work to put our "disordered" flesh back under control:

The education of the conscience is a lifelong task. From the earliest years, it awakens the child to the knowledge and practice of the interior law recognized by conscience. Prudent education teaches virtue; it prevents or cures fear, selfishness and pride, resentment arising from guilt, and feelings of complacency, born of human weakness and faults. The education of the conscience guarantees freedom and engenders peace of heart. (CCC 1784)

Parents have to take an interest in their children; they have to be controlled and helped and not just placed in front of the television. They have to be delicate and discreet in dealing with their children—but also firm when necessary. Children must be taught the difference between right and wrong as well as respect for others. All of this needs to be adapted to the needs of the child, and they particularly need guidance in self-control. By teaching them the social graces they become more civilised, and this makes them more receptive spiritually too.

The fruitfulness of conjugal love extends to the fruits of the moral, spiritual, and supernatural life that parents hand on to their children by education. Parents are the principal and first educators of their children. In this sense the fundamental task of marriage and family is to be at the service of life. (CCC 1653)

Parents should live their vocation with their children rather than ask them if they want to become a Priest or religious. They should pick this up from their parents quite naturally and never be asked, since this might well lead to resentment. We shouldn't spoil our children with too much of anything; they need everything in moderation. All of us are responsible for this. Those children who are brought up in an atmosphere of love have an ideal environment. Children have a very deep faith in their parents, but this mustn't be abused.

At First Communion they should be clearly taught that it is Jesus they receive; skill and tact are needed to present this, so pray to the Lord of the harvest for teachers to explain this, and for their parents to understand their role too. We have to build on the beautiful natural virtues of nobility, tenderness, and faithfulness, consecrating and developing them by, and through, grace. We can get children to join in the Rosary, even if it is only the first decade: they shouldn't be asked to do too much:

> The Christian family is a communion of persons, a sign and image of the communion of the Father and the Son in the Holy Spirit. In the procreation and education of children it reflects the Father's work of creation. It is called to partake of the prayer and sacrifice of Christ. Daily prayer and the reading of the Word of God strengthen it in charity. The Christian family has an evangelizing and missionary task. (CCC 2205)

Some fathers don't know how to hold a child; it's usually easier for mothers. If we know how to be tender with children, and they trust our tenderness, then we are making progress. We should seek the right atmosphere for children— don't take chances with holidays or friendships. This means christianizing our thoughts and actions, not putting children in danger, or being negligent. For adults, too, some friendships are good others bad. We have to respect our friends but not allow our lives to become full of superficial things, such as television.

Fatherhood and the Family

Children are looking for the truth as much as their parents; and they can often be more aware of it. Parents need to prove their love to their children; if you are away then write to them or phone. They must strive to impress the child with their compassion for them. Parents also have to be prepared to forgive their children or risk losing them. Children can suffer by not being loved sufficiently by their parents—but God is able to compensate for this. There are problems today with broken homes; God can give the necessary sensitivity to deal compassionately with such delicate situations. People suffering like this are the beloved children of the Church. In this situation it's difficult to speak about a loving Father in heaven, when they haven't experienced this on earth—what can we say to them? We should spend time with people like this, those without much experience of love and care.

One of Marthe's intuitions concerned the role of the father as being the one who draws out his children: the same is true for the Father of a community, such as a Foyer.

So we shouldn't think we are superior to others; we have to look to provide all the little details of love which are so important in all relationships. We need to try and encourage an interior feeling in the child for discerning the will of God. Children should be allowed to make decisions and choose things for themselves; they should be taught to be sensitive to God's will. With small children we should speak only for a short time on religious matters and then with much respect. Children need their parents' gentleness and goodness. We are asked to enter into the great mystery of God. We should talk to children about all this and put great emphasis on family prayer, taking the child's temperament into account. We must concentrate on the essentials. It isn't easy to educate children now—much compassion is needed:

> The fecundity of conjugal love cannot be reduced solely to the procreation of children, but must extend to their moral education and their spiritual formation. 'The role of parents in education is of such importance that it is almost impossible to provide an adequate substitute.' The right and the duty of parents to educate their children are primordial and inalienable. (CCC 2221)

The family is the domestic Church, and both it and other communities face pressures which cause its disruption, but it can be reunited through Christ. The Holy Spirit is in the hearts of little children—this is a real mystery in the Church. Children respond to the Eucharist, Christ's living and life-giving presence as living bread. When we read Scripture to children we should emphasize that it is Jesus who says this or that. At the other end of the spectrum, we shouldn't judge our parents, who have given us life, and it is obviously wrong to abandon one's parents.

We can have a communion with nature and other people through ordinary gestures. Eating is a type of "communion" with food. Man's work involves communion with the earth and soil in growing things—ideally, we shouldn't have to buy potatoes!

Marriage and Consecrated Life

> The matrimonial covenant, by which a man and a woman establish between themselves a partnership of the whole of life, is by its nature ordered toward the good of the spouses and the procreation and education of offspring; this covenant between baptized persons has been raised by Christ the Lord to the dignity of a sacrament. (CCC 1601)

One of the main sins of omission in married life is not to properly care for the other—each day has to be lived in tenderness. Husbands and wives should love each other as Christ loved the Church. The wife should be in submission to her husband since he represents and expresses Christ in the family. St Paul wrote to the church in Corinth, speaking of the need for people to make sacrifices in order to achieve unity between couples, families, and indeed the whole community. As the *Catechism* states: "... marriage helps to overcome self-absorption, egoism, pursuit of one's own pleasure, and to open oneself to the other, to mutual aid and to self-giving." (1609)

It is difficult for married couples to be fully attached to both families, so there may be times when people have to be adult enough to say "no" to unreasonable demands. Internal problems between the couple don't need their parents interfering unnecessarily. Also, there can be differences in temperament; that is, the woman can be more insightful, and this has to be acknowledged. Before marriage, couples should go on retreat in preparation: they need to really understand each other, and not just be concerned about surface appearances. This will help people to be mature enough to live for each other. Preparation for marriage starts very early, even in childhood. Married love involves a gift of self; it is also a blueprint for other forms of love.

Sterility can be a product of internal stress, and perhaps the gift of children isn't given in such cases. Stresses in marriage can prevent its full fruitfulness. All the women who carry a child must realise that there is a new being, a new person in their womb. There is an unconscious bond between the unborn child and the parents, which is not just a physical thing.

All abortion is a crime:

> Human life must be respected and protected absolutely from the moment of conception. From the first moment of his existence, a human being must be recognized as having the rights of a person—among which is the inviolable right of every innocent being to life. (CCC 2270)

We should pray for abortionists, rather than frighten them; try to change them, help them.

The Image of God is found in community and also in nuptial love. Foyer life is family life where the community is called into being through the grace of God; but even community life can be difficult with its own temptations and problems. It is a long job to create community, and there are bound to be tensions which have to be dealt with. St Paul's advice is to make up differences and have the same spirit. Aberrations that exist in relationships are mainly due to the failure of people to give themselves wholly.

The marriage at Cana was the first sign given in the Gospels, and so has a deep symbolic meaning as regards marriage in general. Married, single and consecrated life all involve different types of love. Consecrated life demands absolute fidelity as does married life, although they can both become stale and "cut off." In either form, the individual is called to an intensity of love, a total gift of self. We become possessed by the one we love.

The Catholic faith as a whole is logical; for example, divorced people can't receive Communion since they are no longer true witnesses of the love of Christ: but they can still offer themselves by coming to Mass.

Society and Other People

The human person needs to live in society. Society is not for him an extraneous addition but a requirement of his nature. Through the exchange with others, mutual service and dialogue with his brethren, man develops his potential; he thus responds to his vocation. (CCC 1879)

The ability to know how to receive or accept the "other," the person who is spiritually or physically hungry, is something we must develop. We discover the face of Jesus through the other. When we have accepted the other, when we have looked at the person before us as someone unique, someone who is beyond the material, then in the ordinary actions of the day— such as the breaking of bread the disciples at Emmaus experienced—our eyes are opened. This is the way we learn and grow, accepting the pain and suffering of life as well as death itself. Prayer will help us to see the person of Christ in the other, but without this we can't really advance. He loves us and has died for us; once we truly realise this we can give up earthly things with joy. As Marthe repeatedly said, our life is worth what our prayer is worth; without this attitude we will not understand the true meaning of suffering and death.

We must respect people as they are. We must develop our minds and be open to new insights. Modern thinking fails to acknowledge God. How can we combat this? It is difficult, but we have to start to let God work in us gently, so that we can be a sign for others. We should take ourselves seriously and so go towards other people in an attempt to understand them, and then teach them about God. We should realize that we have "charisms" which will lead people to God, for example, the work of hospital or prison chaplains. However we mustn't think we have all the answers—that leads to pride and self-satisfaction. We should have a fatherly and understanding · approach to others. We need to interiorize and enrich ourselves; then we will be open to others and see all people as equal. Prayer helps us to do this and we will be filled with unbelievable strength.

People in poorer countries often have more time for others; God calls the poor; their hearts are more open—the rich aren't so giving. We also have to take time for human contacts which are real and not superficial; such contact isn't satisfying for people. Cohesion between people grows in silence and over time. We don't give enough time to other people or to God. We must change this. We have to find our own way of being with Jesus and learn to respect the other person's way if this is different. We mustn't judge unbelievers.

Man is meant to complete creation—but without undue obsession. Man is the center of creation and God has done everything through, in, and with Christ so that we get all things, including our very being from Him. Man is only truly man through his relationship with God.

We are invited to work in the world by God, but we mustn't be like the rich man in the Gospel who wanted to build bigger barns—he forgot the essential thing. He forgot his soul.

We should look after our relatives but distinguish between their needs and caprices. Similarly, we should visit our neighbours in order to understand their problems; the life of Christ has been given to us from the Father, to the Son, and then through the Church, in order that all people may be reached. This is the overwhelming obligation we have—to announce the Gospel of Christ. The virtue of charity is a movement of the heart, like gravitation attracting a stone to the earth: man's heart is made to love and so baptised Christians should rush to help others.

The Apparition at Mamre to Abraham

And the Lord appeared to him by the oaks of Mamre, as he sat at the door of his tent in the heat of the day. He lifted up his eyes and looked, and behold, three men stood in front of him. When he saw them, he ran from the tent door to meet them, and bowed himself to the earth, and said, "My lord, if I have found favor in your sight, do not pass by your servant. Let a little water be brought, and wash your feet, and rest yourselves under the tree, while I fetch a morsel of bread, that you may refresh yourselves, and after that you may pass on—since you have come to your servant." So they said, "Do as you have said."

And Abraham hastened into the tent to Sarah, and said, "Make ready quickly three measures of fine meal, knead it, and make cakes." And Abraham ran to the herd, and took a calf, tender and good, and gave it to the servant, who hastened to prepare it. Then he took curds, and milk, and the calf which he had prepared, and set it before them; and he stood by them under the tree while they ate. (Gen 18:1-8)

Rublev's famous icon of the Trinity represents the three divine persons, or angels, who appeared to Abraham at Mamre. We see Abraham resting physically but he was meditating in his heart on the promise God had made to him of many descendants. He was old, but as yet had no children; he was thinking deeply about all this, letting himself be worked upon, when the three "men" appeared before him. Abraham took an immediate interest in these strangers and hurried to offer them hospitality. There is a lesson here for us as Christians: we can be too egotistical to care about other people unless they are of interest to us in some way, but Abraham was different, he offered the best of himself and his goods to his guests.

The missionary who announces the Gospel needs to be poor and humble, but also aware of his "richness" in that he has the immense honour of announcing the Word of God. Only the Holy Spirit, though, can really touch hearts. There is a great problem of poverty in the world. Social development lags behind economic development. There is a big gulf between the rich and the poor which is constantly growing. The rich are getting richer at the expense of a larger number of poorer people. We need to change the basic structures of these societies to challenge the vested interests of the rich. The poor live the Gospel in a natural way—they live in utter dependence on God. Material poverty doesn't stop poor churches being full of joy: this is just the opposite to the situation found in the West.

The great majority of Catholics are in the developing world. How we can we help them to become more incorporated in the Church? There is a problem if communities are too politicized without being evangelized. There is a need for integration here. There is also a very real danger in confronting the rich; bridges need to be built between the two sections of society. The Catholic population is dropping in some developing countries as Protestant sects gain ground. The problem with this sort of Protestantism is that it is often a form of escapism which isn't rooted in real life. It doesn't try to change the social order and so it is left to the Catholic Church to try and do this.

15

Sin, Temptation, Illness & Death

Sin is an offense against reason, truth, and right conscience; it is failure in genuine love for God and neighbor caused by a perverse attachment to certain goods. It wounds the nature of man and injures human solidarity. It has been defined as "an utterance, a deed, or a desire contrary to the eternal law." (CCC 1849)

When deep suffering strikes others we have to help. We have a Christian duty to pray: where two or three pray and ask for God's help, He can work wonders. Today many people are afflicted by compulsions such as drug addiction or alcoholism, which are, practically, beyond their strength to combat. Marthe insisted that we have to think about all this and do what we can to help. How do we explain the sorrow of so many evil things which are happening in the world, or the concentration camps of the Second World War? These seem to point to more than just human inactivity or mistakes—we need to look for the deeper reasons.

We feel the heaviness of our sinfulness and this is something which has to be faced. People are becoming more doubting and fixed on themselves; but as Christians we are meant to move away from that and become something new and different. We are often like the Pharisee who thought he was better than the Publican. The disorder which keeps us down, our sinfulness, doesn't stop the mercy of God acting on a person who turns to Him. We need to enter into this concretely, judging ourselves critically, but without becoming bitter. We gain experience as we get older but this doesn't necessarily make us wiser. Despite our sinfulness we still have a need, and even a desire, to praise God. St Augustine said that God has made us for Himself and we cannot be satisfied until we rest in Him, this God who is great and infinitely worthy of praise.

Sin is the destruction that man has brought on himself and it most affects us when we don't respond to our vocation. The only sin which can't be forgiven is the sin against the Holy Spirit, that is, obstinate pride and a denial of the truth. We can see the possibilities within the heart of Man, from extreme goodness to extreme evil—anything is possible. The revolt of the devil is the cause of evil, of pride, through his refusal to serve. The existence of hell is certain, but we don't know the identity of those who are there.

Christ manifests the tenderness of the Father to us; He heals us of our illness, our sin, at a deep level. People who want to grow in faith must desire new and greater things. It is a problem to feel that God isn't listening to us but we need to grow beyond that. We shouldn't be satisfied with what we have—we must go beyond, raising our eyes higher, if we are to really achieve anything. We can run after mirages but the Word of God helps us to go beyond our feelings.

The Fall of Man

Now the serpent was more subtle than any other wild creature that the Lord God had made. He said to the woman, "Did God say, 'You shall not eat of any tree of the garden'?" And the woman said to the serpent, "We may eat of the fruit of the trees of the garden; but God said, 'You shall not eat of the fruit of the tree which is in the midst of the garden, neither shall you touch it, lest you die.'" But the serpent said to the woman, "You will not die. For God knows that when you eat of it your eyes will be opened, and you will be like God, knowing good and evil."

So when the woman saw that the tree was good for food, and that it was a delight to the eyes, and that the tree was to be desired to make one wise, she took of its fruit and ate; and she also gave some to her husband, and he ate. Then the eyes of both were opened, and they knew that they were naked; and they sewed fig leaves together and made themselves aprons. (Gen 3:1-7)

Genesis gives us an exact definition of sin; man wanting to be self-sufficient. This revolt against God has deeply wounded man's soul. Sin led to the loss of eternal life; it adversely marked our nature, intelligence, will and freedom.

The first man was not only created good, but was also established in friendship with his Creator and in harmony with himself and with the creation around him, in a state that would be surpassed only by the glory of the new creation in Christ. The Church, interpreting the symbolism of biblical language in an authentic way, in the light of the New Testament and Tradition, teaches that our first parents, Adam and Eve, were constituted in an original "state of holiness and justice". This grace of original holiness was "to share in ... divine life". ... The account of the fall in Genesis 3 uses figurative language, but affirms a primeval event, a deed that took place at the beginning of the history of man. Revelation gives us the certainty of faith that the whole of human history is marked by the original fault freely committed by our first parents. (CCC 374, 375, 390)

The story of the Fall of Man embodies great truths. The nature of a serpent is evil and hypocritical, a wily animal; the devil insinuates himself into everything. This account doesn't mean that women are lesser beings. Man is in charge of creation but there is one restriction: he mustn't eat the fruit of the tree of life. Why was there such a restriction? This image reveals the beauty of God's total gift to us; He has given us everything but we don't own creation. This restriction emphasised its nature as a gift for which man should have been thankful.

We need to look at the deeper meaning of the text and beware of rationalistic explanations. We must accept, understand and hear the Word of God humbly. God wishes us to accept things as they are; we need the heart of a child to really understand these things and can't do this without lowliness of heart. If we only take an earthly approach to this particular passage we won't understand it. The prohibition against eating from the tree was meant as a sign of man's obedience to God. Through our obedience to God, we give Him praise and glory and so give meaning to our actions. God is at the heart of our freedom, our liberty and our being. He respects us, and although we are free, we can't be totally sovereign and independent: we are still dependent on God.

Adam and Eve died spiritually; they no longer had a supernatural relationship with God, but they still retained their dignity as persons and were still above the animals. The woman responded to the serpent and this was the prelude to the first sin, which was presented as freedom, as becoming like God. The serpent appealed to mankind's wish to be independent of God, but this is impossible. It is a sign of senseless pride to think this can happen. By talking with the demon, Eve already doubted God; we too shouldn't entertain his temptations. Pride makes us take our talents to ourselves, rather than acknowledging that all comes from God. This hubris, this spirit of independence, is also a spirit of death. Often, people moving away from God have destructive experiences, with drugs, or even temptations to commit suicide.

The devil was trying to undermine God's authority, trying to break His relationship with man. Once God is suppressed and the person becomes totally dependent on self we become self-destructive. If our sonship is broken we become narcissistic. The woman saw the fruit of the tree as good to eat and pleasing to the eye; she offered it to her husband. We can find an explanation for all the negative aspects of civilization here, and it greatly helps us to understand human behaviour, family life, education, and so on. We have taken the fruit to ourselves—we rejoice in ourselves, not God and this leads to eternal death. The eyes of both of them were opened, they knew they were naked, alone, and selfish, an obstacle to themselves. This was the start of disorder in the life of mankind, a cutting of the dependency on God, signified by their shame at their nakedness.

The Consequences of Original Sin

Amongst the consequences of original sin are the concupiscence of the eyes and the body: we look too much to things outside of ourselves, things which satisfy our instincts, that is, food, drink, sleep, and so on. We have to be aware of these tendencies. The wounding of our intellect and will power, caused by original sin, means we find it difficult to judge the difference between right and wrong in concrete situations. So we have a lack of fine judgment, and this is something which needs to be developed.

> And they heard the sound of the Lord God walking in the garden in the cool of the day, and the man and his wife hid themselves from the presence of the Lord God among the trees of the garden. But the Lord God called to the man, and said to him, "Where are you?" And he said, "I heard the sound of thee in the garden, and I was afraid, because I was naked; and I hid myself." He said, "Who told you that you were naked? Have you eaten of the tree of which I commanded you not to eat?"
>
> The man said, "The woman whom thou gavest to be with me, she gave me fruit of the tree, and I ate." Then the Lord God said to the woman, "What is this that you have done?" The woman said, "The serpent beguiled me, and I ate." The Lord God said to the serpent, "Because you have done this, cursed are you above all cattle, and above all wild animals; upon your belly you shall go, and dust you shall eat all the days of your life. I will put enmity between you and the woman, and between your seed and her seed; he shall bruise your head, and you shall bruise his heel." (Gen 3:8-15)

Adam and Eve heard God in the garden and hid themselves. God called to them—this is an indication of the way God never abandons us. The man was afraid so he hid; the man had become spiritually naked. Even when the relationship with Man was broken, God continued to call. This rupture also affects relationships between men and women; they can't fulfil family or social responsibilities. Adam blamed Eve, and we can tend to blame others or society for our own faults. The woman blamed the serpent. The loss of union with God also leads to a loss of union with our fellow men and women, leading to all sorts of other problems.

This passage can help us to understand the reality of sin and our need for a proper relationship with God. He doesn't need us; the Trinity is all sufficient, but God wanted to create beings who could enter into a real relationship with Him. Lamentably, we have become cut off from God through original sin, and our own sins, and alienated by means of pride. We need to open our hearts and spirits to the history of the Church in the world. We must get to know the teaching of the Doctors of the Church, a teaching which is completely opposed to the way the world is acting today. There is a spirit of independence in the world, a spirit of self-sufficiency and indeed selfishness. Even Christians are affected by this—we can wish for things to be different when we know what God really requires. Simpler people understand this more easily; they have a more natural dependence on God. So we must enlighten our minds and desire to be raised up, giving thanks to God.

> To the woman he said, "I will greatly multiply your pain in childbearing; in pain you shall bring forth children, yet your desire shall be for your husband, and he shall rule over you." And to Adam he said, "Because you have listened to the voice of your wife, and have eaten of the tree of which I commanded you, 'You shall not eat of it,' cursed is the ground because of you; in toil you shall eat of it all the days of your life; thorns and thistles it shall bring forth to you; and you shall eat the plants of

the field. In the sweat of your face you shall eat bread till you return to the ground, for out of it you were taken; you are dust, and to dust you shall return." (Gen 3:16-19)

The hostility between men and women, and between humans and the lower animals, was a consequence of the Fall. Mary is the new Woman who was foretold in Genesis; as was the battle between her offspring and that of the devil. The offspring of the Woman is Christ, who is our head and has saved us from the disobedience of the first sin—He had to suffer and die on the Cross for our sakes.

The Mystery of Evil

For the wrath of God is revealed from heaven against all ungodliness and wickedness of men who by their wickedness suppress the truth. For what can be known about God is plain to them, because God has shown it to them. Ever since the creation of the world his invisible nature, namely, his eternal power and deity, has been clearly perceived in the things that have been made. So they are without excuse; for although they knew God they did not honor him as God or give thanks to him, but they became futile in their thinking and their senseless minds were darkened.

Claiming to be wise, they became fools, and exchanged the glory of the immortal God for images resembling mortal man or birds or animals or reptiles. Therefore God gave them up in the lusts of their hearts to impurity, to the dishonoring of their bodies among themselves, because they exchanged the truth about God for a lie and worshiped and served the creature rather than the Creator, who is blessed for ever! Amen.

For this reason God gave them up to dishonorable passions. Their women exchanged natural relations for unnatural, and the men likewise gave up natural relations with women and were consumed with passion for one another, men committing shameless acts with men and receiving in their own persons the due penalty for their error. And since they did not see fit to acknowledge God, God gave them up to a base mind and to improper conduct.

They were filled with all manner of wickedness, evil, covetousness, malice. Full of envy, murder, strife, deceit, malignity, they are gossips, slanderers, haters of God, insolent, haughty, boastful, inventors of evil, disobedient to parents, foolish, faithless, heartless, ruthless. Though they know God's decree that those who do such things deserve to die, they not only do them but approve those who practice them. (Romans 1:18-32)

The impiety and depravity of man is a mystery but there isn't really a valid excuse for all this since God's existence should be acknowledged. Because of a lack of concern for the truth sinners give up the divine truth for a lie. This leads to unnatural passions and all sorts of evils. This terrifying passage shows us what slavery to the passions really is. St Paul was exasperated by the stupidity and sinfulness of those around him. The heart of the problem is man's revolt against God, his resistance towards the Creator. St Paul described God as the invisible power whose existence is proved by the whole of creation; and so there was really no excuse for this sinful behaviour. The darkening of the mind experienced by those around him was due to their rejection of God; they became unreasonable and closed their minds to reality. They then became idolaters, denigrating both themselves and God. He then left them in their own impurity to dishonor their bodies. This in turn led to unnatural sexual practices, including homosexuality. Paul then listed a whole series of perversions and evil passions which had resulted from this rejection of God.

In His goodness, God decided to create us, and when we went wrong to save us. He chastened us by allowing the world to fall into sin, a sin which has badly affected God's gifts. Original sin becomes our own through our sins, but we have the promise and reality of salvation given to the Woman and her Seed. We need to approach all this in humility, we need Mary's influence to understand these things. Even she and Joseph didn't fully understand Jesus' role, as, for example, when He was lost for three days, before being found in the Temple. So we need to try to understand God's way and seek fulfilment, entering into a proper relationship with Him, a relationship of love. There is an intrinsic need for man to respect God; we die spiritually if we try to get away from God. But man is continually being cared for and called back by God who leads us to Himself.

Temptation

The Holy Spirit makes us discern between trials, which are necessary for the growth of the inner man, and temptation, which leads to sin and death. We must also discern between being tempted and consenting to temptation. Finally, discernment unmasks the lie of temptation, whose object appears to be good, a "delight to the eyes" and desirable, when in reality its fruit is death. (CCC 2847)

At the beginning of His ministry Jesus was filled with the Spirit and led into the desert, where He was tempted for forty days. The New Adam confronted the devil; He was pushed by the Spirit to renounce His divine advantage and be like us, in order to expiate our sins. From a human point of view this was a mission He couldn't accomplish on His own, and so He was filled by the Spirit and led into the wilderness. Jesus made himself poor, small and indigent in the depths of His heart. The devil tempted Him, almost making fun of Him. He tried to make Jesus compromise by accepting that he was partly right in refusing to serve the Father, in rebelling. This rebellion of the fallen angels is the reason for hell. We must remember that we can go to hell if we misuse our will power—we are ultimately responsible for where we will spend eternity.

Illness and Death

Illness and suffering have always been among the gravest problems confronted in human life. In illness, man experiences his powerlessness, his limitations, and his finitude. Every illness can make us glimpse death. (CCC 1500)

We can offer our sufferings and illnesses to God, but unfortunately we often find it difficult to see God's presence in our own problems; we can feel that God has withdrawn from us. If a Christian is ill, then, according to St Paul, the whole Church is ill. The Lord also allows us to have illnesses as a way of warning us to change our lives. Jesus looked after the sick and dying; this is an important ministry in the Church. Paradoxically, it can also bring peace and joy, since everyone is then useful, and we stay close to the Cross of Christ.

What is really serious in life? Death is something in the distance—but it is inevitable. Marthe lived for her death, so she could be "welcomed into the arms of her heavenly Father" and enter His kingdom. This is something we need to prepare for in life. Death is, in a certain sense, the aim of life, the way to reach eternal life, but also the time when we are most savagely attacked by the demon. We can lose the use of our senses—it is a dangerous juncture and the most crucial moment of our life.

We can die any time—we must be fully aware of this. It is the time to make the greatest act of love of our life. God calls the person to himself and we must prepare for this meeting. We have the reassurance of the Holy Spirit, and Mary, to welcome us. As in the struggle of Jesus' agony, the mortally sick person is often still able to hear and understand, despite appearances. We should make acts of charity for persons in their last moments; their last breath will bring them to God. A person in purgatory is in a state of penance, waiting for deliverance; they can't merit anything; merit can only be gained on earth.

There is the temptation of nothingness after death; but the arms of the Father are there to hold us. Everyone has to live this one day—and we need to think about it seriously. We should continue to pray for half an hour after the apparent time of a person's "death." Marthe seemed to indicate that there is a period between the "apparent" and "real" death of a person. We mustn't judge when people commit suicide—leave that to God. It is a sin against the Spirit, to consider life as one's own property to be disposed of. This is often a terrible temptation; we should pray for those afflicted in this way and for those who do kill themselves.

Meditate on death but don't terrorize people who are dying. Nowadays people don't want to talk about it. There are sad events such as the death of children which have to be coped with. But we must realize that despite the sadness of aspects of life God wanted creation otherwise we wouldn't be here. All aspects of creation are meant to praise God. We must respect the unborn and the aged—that means no abortion or euthanasia. Everyone is worthy of respect.

16

Suffering & the Cross of Christ

The eternal desire of God is that we are predestined for salvation; this cost Him the price of His death on the Cross—it cost Him dearly. Friday is the particular day when we think of the mystery of Redemption and the Cross. We should look at sin from above; from the point of view of mercy. Suffering can often lead to great insights in prayer, as in the case of Marthe, and during periods of sleeplessness we can think about all this as she did. We are redeemed through Jesus' blood. Only Jesus crucified matters and not the wisdom of the world.

Jesus solemnized the Jewish Passover. The ardor of Jesus to eat the Passover before suffering is described: "And when the hour came, he sat at table, and the apostles with Him. And he said to them, 'I have earnestly desired to eat this Passover with you before I suffer; for I tell you I shall not eat it until it is fulfilled in the kingdom of God.' " (Luke 22:14-16)

The origin of Jesus' ardor is in His need to do His Father's will and accomplish the work He was given by the Father. We need to meditate on this ardor. The agony of Christ was a struggle which had a terrible effect on the heart of Mary. We read in St Luke's Gospel about the mystery of Judas' betrayal of Jesus, and must think about how this must have greatly increased His agony.

And he came out, and went, as was his custom, to the Mount of Olives; and the disciples followed him. And when he came to the place he said to them, "Pray that you may not enter into temptation." And he withdrew from them about a stone's throw, and knelt down and prayed, "Father, if thou art willing, remove this cup from me; nevertheless not my will, but thine, be done." And when he rose from prayer, he came to the disciples and found them sleeping for sorrow, and he said to them, "Why do you sleep? Rise and pray that you may not enter into temptation." (Luke 22:39-46)

The agony in the garden is found in all four Gospels, but Luke leaves out some of the things said by the other evangelists. It involved a terrible tearing in the soul of Jesus, and shows us that prayer is necessary to avoid temptation and destruction. Jesus was ardent before but now He was in anguish. He prayed to His Father. A deep Christian life will always bring a cross which must be accepted and borne. Jesus went through severe trials as we sometimes have to. The sweat of blood in the garden was lived by Marthe through her stigmata. The important point is our insertion into the life of the Trinity through the Cross of Christ. The work of redemption is greater than that of creation—this tremendously important work was the reason for Jesus' ardor.

The Effects of Suffering

By suffering prayerfully, and in silence, we can change people, influencing them by hidden means and example. God converts them through our prayer and sacrifice: conversions are not dependant on our intelligence. We shouldn't be afraid to speak of Jesus' sufferings to others. Jesus wanted to be so like us that He was prepared to undergo His Passion as man. But the tenderness of the Father forgives us. The eternal life we aspire to is only won at the price of suffering, as it was for Jesus. Our sacrifice in this is a privilege, and part of our vocation. Unless we go to the depths of this, we remain on the threshold, and don't really understand the Cross as Marthe understood it. This means letting the thoughts and feelings of Our Lord permeate our minds and hearts. We must nourish our hearts with good thoughts, in order to be a sign of love and light; we find all this in the Gospel but it is difficult work.

Thus, we have to enter into the mystery of the Heart of Jesus to truly understand and experience the Cross. The Gospels which describe the Passion are overwhelming; Jesus as Son didn't want to cling to the beatific vision. His role also involved helping His Mother to make her ultimate sacrifice. All this is part of our faith—it's not a question of having to prove it. We must take our time over this and pray about it at our own pace, being guided by the Holy Spirit. In contemplating Jesus' Cross we may feel nothing, but we can't control our feelings. We need to try, though, to attain the tenderness and admiration St Paul felt for Jesus crucified. There is nothing greater than the sacrifice of Jesus Christ.

We have to give our attention to what is being taught—it isn't an outwardly beautiful thing we are contemplating, but we have to try to enter into the spirit of the Passion and see its inner beauty. We are strengthened by the Passion. We need to contemplate it with all our powers—heart, mind and soul. This means becoming like St Ignatius of Loyola, someone who was deeply in love with Christ's Passion and in touch with His sufferings. We tend not to want to get close to the sufferings of Christ; we turn away to look at other things rather than accepting Jesus' love for us in His Passion. We need to recognise the spirit and not just the letter; not judge exteriorly but rather look at the heart of Christ.

The wisdom of the world doesn't recognise God and we need His wisdom to really understand the Cross. When St Paul was in Athens, its intellectuals and leaders didn't understand the Cross; they thought the whole thing was foolishness. St Thérèse of the Child Jesus also embraced the Cross and chose the hard life of Carmel with all its tensions— but her love of the Cross brought her through all that. She understood the mystery of the Cross and drew strength from it.

Jesus is one person with two natures. He took on the consequence of being human, but without all the consequences of original sin: He wasn't subject to concupiscence. He underwent His terrible sufferings for us and is the first of a multitude of the resurrected. On the way of the Cross, one word, one thought, one drop of blood, would have been enough to save the world. So He renounced all His advantages and was obedient to the will of the Father. In the garden He said He would accept the Father's will and so He was given a name above all names.

The love of Jesus' human heart for us led Him to refuse to avoid suffering; He wanted to expiate sin for us. It is astonishing that He should do this; we can't imagine how much He suffered—and the same holds for His Mother and for those who have followed His path of affliction, like Marthe. The demonic powers of the devil affected all the apostles; they were frightened and ran away. There was a constant fight in the Heart of Jesus; He was greatly anguished by the ingratitude of mankind. The more we grow spiritually, the more we are tempted; this isn't a consoling thought, but it is logical and is something we have to face.

It is an honor to do God's work, but it isn't always easy. We face difficulties and other souls need the offering of our life: but often we just don't make the effort. Marthe was terribly concerned about the millions of people around the world who didn't know Christ. The Father won't give us glory in heaven unless we have earned it. Jesus suffered and so must we, despite this being painful for us. This is the authentic doctrine of St Paul, who said that our Baptism had raised us to a new life and so we should look to spiritual things. We have been plunged into the blood of Christ and so our lives are now hidden with Christ in God. Our real life will be manifested at the resurrection. In our consciousness of being raised up, we need to continue, to keep going, seeking the things above. We will certainly find ourselves being crucified if we do all this.

Marthe and the Passion

When we read the Passion of Jesus, as described by Marthe, we can see a conformity with the writings of other mystics. Marthe saw Jesus as being alone with Mary before the Passion, preparing her for her role in His work with gratitude and filial devotion. He told her all that would be fulfilled in Jerusalem, all the plots He would suffer, although she had been somewhat prepared by her reading of the prophecies. But she had to be initiated more directly into Jesus' sacrifice, as she had a crucial part to fulfil in the plan of the Eternal Father, in uniting her sufferings with those of her divine Son. She had to be one with Him as Co-Redemptrix. Jesus explained, from the depths of His human heart, how she had been called to co-operate in God's plan from all eternity. Jesus had agreed to offer Himself fully; now Mary was to be asked to make her contribution to the final part of the mystery of our redemption. She accepted her role with humility and love, giving her full consent.

But despite Jesus' delicate preparation of her she still felt her soul torn with anguish as the Passion approached. He promised to live with her in the Eucharist, and told her it was better for all that things should happen this way. Jesus told Mary that their union would be more complete once the Passion and Resurrection were completed. He consoled His Mother fully.

It is important for human relationships to be marked by tangible signs, but they must be sincere, from the heart. Marthe's intuition was to describe all the details of the relationship between Jesus and Mary. Jesus also told His Mother of her immense role in the future of the Church, a role of encouraging the Apostles, advising and sustaining them. She would help them in their weakness and encourage them in the way of the Cross. He spoke about Peter and his great faith; about John who represented love and how she would be a mother to him, and he a tender and loving son.

Peter and John were preparing for the Passover at this time while Judas was making his traitorous plans. Marthe also spoke about the love of Martha and Mary Magdalene for Jesus. Marthe's text shows us how we must show love in all its little details—the slightest lack of charity will show. The Blessed Virgin didn't weep much at this stage, but she was terribly sad and recollected. Jesus consoled and embraced her, thanking her for the care she had given Him, all her maternal solicitude. John was to replace Jesus as her son. Marthe saw all this by an interior vision, illuminated by the Holy Spirit. Marthe described the beauty of the relationship between Jesus and Mary; but we do have to be careful of adding too much detail in an apocryphal manner. Marthe chose those details she felt should be revealed under the influence of the Spirit. We can't see them as another Gospel; they need the approval of the Church before they can be published.

Jesus was now entering into the period of His most heroic submission to the will of His Father. The time of fulfilment was near and Jesus fully accepted everything He would have to suffer. Mary's will was for the service of God; she was totally without sin and displayed an unheard of strength in carrying out God's will. So Mary wept and was again consoled by Jesus—imagine the love in that last conversation between the Son and the Mother! Jesus told Mary He would spend the Last Supper with her spiritually, before leaving Bethany, full of sadness, to take part in His last Passover.

In the upper room, Jesus told His disciples they would face persecution; if the world persecuted Him then they too would have to suffer. He told them that the world only loved its own, but that He had drawn them away from the world. These words applied to all the early Christians, the martyrs of both sexes who would bear witness to Jesus: we too can face suffering and trial. Jesus then recollected himself and broke the bread. At that moment, it seemed to Marthe that Mary received Communion spiritually, although she couldn't really explain this. She saw her enter the room very quickly and receive the host before disappearing. This seemed like a very striking thing to Marthe—she saw this scene many times, as she relived the Passion every week.

Jesus left the Eucharist as the most outstanding reality for those who love Him; a living reality, His flesh and blood under the appearance of bread and wine, made eternal for us.

John gave Mary communion alone after the Resurrection. This was a feast in the early Church, a feast of great joy for the Apostles. Mary's holy and immaculate soul was magnificently divinized in love. She saw Jesus in her heart, through an interior vision, penetrating the substance and adoring Him as a small child, as she had adored Him throughout her life. Mary thought again of the Passion at this moment during Communion, right up to the end of her life. She could now accept this because she knew her mission had been completed—thanks to Jesus, all of humanity could now be saved.

Mary was the new Ark of the Covenant, and much more precious than the old Ark venerated by the Israelites. She is the Immaculate One, without the least sin, the Mother of God and our mother. Jesus rested in her soul and Mary relived their intimacy of life during Communion. We can't really understand the intimate communion of Mary with Jesus—her love for Him and her humility. Even so, the joy of Mary was not complete; she was still separated from Jesus, and possessed Him without seeing Him. Something was missing and she waited quietly for death. St Paul said He wanted to die to be with Jesus: one of the graces of the Eucharist is to enable us to draw nearer to eternal life, to desire eternity.

At each Communion Mary felt a burning desire to be fully with Jesus. Her constant thought was on the supreme beatitude of heaven. It should be the same for us—the more fervent our Communions, the better for us. If only we could have Mary's thoughts and feelings when receiving the Eucharist! Before Communion we should ask Mary to prepare our hearts—indeed, we need Communion because we don't love our brothers enough. Then we should make our thanksgiving with Mary, in silence, gentleness, and an expectancy of eternal life. We shouldn't be impassive or discontented; we must cultivate a taste for eternity.

Scriptural Way of the Cross

First Station - Jesus is condemned to death

Pilate went out again, and said to them, "See, I am bringing him out to you, that you may know that I find no crime in him." So Jesus came out, wearing the crown of thorns and the purple robe. Pilate said to them, "Behold the man!" When the chief priests and the officers saw him, they cried out, "Crucify him, crucify him!" (John 19:4-6) So when Pilate saw that he was gaining nothing, but rather that a riot was beginning, he took water and washed his hands before the crowd, saying, "I am innocent of this man's blood; see to it yourselves." And all the people answered, "His blood be on us and on our children!" (Matt 27:24-25)

Second Station - Jesus carries His Cross

So Pilate, wishing to satisfy the crowd, released for them Barabbas; and having scourged Jesus, he delivered him to be crucified ... And when they had mocked him, they stripped him of the purple cloak, and put his own clothes on him. And they led him out to crucify him. (Mark 15:15, 20) So they took Jesus, and he went out, bearing his own cross, to the place called the place of a skull, which is called in Hebrew Golgotha. (John 19:17)

Third Station - Jesus falls for the first time

And [Jesus] said to all, "If any man would come after me, let him deny himself and take up his cross daily and follow me. For whoever would save his life will lose it; and whoever loses his life for my sake, he will save it." (Luke 9:23-24) "Take my yoke upon you, and learn from me; for I am gentle and lowly in heart, and you will find rest for your souls. For my yoke is easy, and my burden is light." (Matt 11:29-30).

Fourth Station - Jesus meets His Mother

[Simeon] took him up in his arms and blessed God and said, "Lord, now lettest thou thy servant depart in peace, according to thy word ..." And his father and his mother marveled at what was said about him; and Simeon blessed them and said to Mary his mother, "Behold, this child is set for the fall and rising of many in Israel, and for a sign that is spoken against (and a sword will pierce through your own soul also), that thoughts out of many hearts may be revealed." (Luke 2:28-29, 33-35)

Fifth Station - Jesus is helped by Simon of Cyrene

And as they led him away, they seized one Simon of Cyrene, who was coming in from the country, and laid on him the cross, to carry it behind Jesus. (Luke 23:26) Now I rejoice in my sufferings for your sake, and in my flesh I complete what is lacking in Christ's afflictions for the sake of his body, that is, the church ... (Col 1:24)

Sixth Station - Jesus' face is wiped by Veronica

As many were astonished at him—his appearance was so marred, beyond human semblance, and his form beyond that of the sons of men—so shall he startle many nations; kings shall shut their mouths because of him; for that which had not been told them they shall see, and that which they have not heard they shall understand. (Isa 52:14-15)

Seventh Station - Jesus falls for the second time

But he was wounded for our transgressions, he was bruised for our iniquities; upon him was the chastisement that made us whole, and with his stripes we are healed. All we like sheep have gone astray; we have turned every one to his own way, and the Lord has laid on him the iniquity of us all. He was oppressed, and he was afflicted, yet he opened not his mouth; like a lamb that is led to the slaughter, and like a sheep that before its shearers is dumb, so he opened not his mouth. (Isa 53:5-7)

Eight Station - Jesus speaks to the women of Jerusalem

And there followed him a great multitude of the people, and of women who bewailed and lamented him. But Jesus turning to them said, "Daughters of Jerusalem, do not weep for me, but weep for yourselves and for your children. ... For if they do this when the wood is green, what will happen when it is dry?" (Luke 23:27-31)

Ninth Station - Jesus falls for the third time

[Jesus], though he was in the form of God, did not count equality with God a thing to be grasped, but emptied himself, taking the form of a servant, being born in the likeness of men. And being found in human form he humbled himself and became obedient unto death, even death on a cross. Therefore God has highly exalted him and bestowed on him the name which is above every name, that at the name of Jesus every knee should bow, in heaven and on earth and under the earth, and every tongue confess that Jesus Christ is Lord, to the glory of God the Father. (Phil 2:6-11)

Tenth Station - Jesus is stripped of His garments

When the soldiers had crucified Jesus they took his garments and made four parts, one for each soldier; also his tunic. But the tunic was without seam, woven from top to bottom; so they said to one another, "Let us not tear it, but cast lots for it to see whose it shall be." This was to fulfil the scripture, "They parted my garments among them, and for my clothing they cast lots." (John 19:23-24) After this Jesus, knowing that all was now finished, said (to fulfil the scripture), "I thirst." A bowl full of vinegar stood there; so they put a sponge full of the vinegar on hyssop and held it to his mouth. (John 19: 28-29)

Eleventh Station - Jesus is nailed to the Cross

And it was the third hour, when they crucified him. And the inscription of the charge against him read, "The King of the Jews." And with him they crucified two robbers, one on his right and one on his left. (Mark 15:25-27) "Yea dogs are round about me; a company of evildoers encircle me; they have pierced my hands and feet—I can count all my bones—they stare and gloat over me ..." (Psalm 22:16-17)

Twelfth Station - Jesus dies on the Cross

"I am poured out like water, and all my bones are out of joint; my heart is like wax; it is melted within my breast; my strength is dried up like a potsherd, and my tongue cleaves to my jaws; thou dost lay me in the dust of death." (Psalm 22:14-15) One of the criminals who were hanged said, "Jesus, remember me when you come into your kingdom." And he said to him, "Truly, I say to you, today you will be with me in Paradise." (Luke 23:39, 42-43) When Jesus saw his mother, and the disciple whom he loved standing near, he said to his mother, "Woman, behold, your son!" Then he said to the disciple, "Behold, your mother!" And from that hour the disciple took her to his own home. (John 19:26-27) Then Jesus, crying with a loud voice, said, "Father, into thy hands I commit my spirit!" And having said this he breathed his last. (Luke 23:46)

Thirteenth Station - Jesus is taken down from the Cross

But one of the soldiers pierced his side with a spear, and at once there came out blood and water. For these things took place that the scripture might be fulfilled, "Not a bone of him shall be broken." And again another scripture says, "They shall look on him whom they have pierced." After this Joseph of Arimathea, who was a disciple of Jesus, but secretly, for fear of the Jews, asked Pilate that he might take away the body of Jesus, and Pilate gave him leave. So he came and took away his body. They took the body of Jesus, and bound it in linen cloths with the spices, as is the burial custom of the Jews. (John 19:34, 36-37, 38, 40)

Fourteenth Station - Jesus is laid in the Sepulcher

And they made his grave with the wicked and with a rich man in his death, although he had done no violence, and there was no deceit in his mouth. (Isa 53:9)

17

The Resurrection &
the New Christian Life

The Resurrection is the keystone of our faith. It is the great triumph of God's power and love. St Paul said that if Christ was not risen then our faith was in vain, without foundation. What is the importance of the Resurrection? Christ took our sin on himself and suffered for us with a definite purpose, so belief in the Resurrection is our fundamental act of faith. Jesus was dead but is now alive with a glorious spiritual life and a body which has, like Mary's, become spiritualized. His Resurrection has power for us and is a model because Jesus was raised due to His obedience to the Father, and not just because He too was God. Because of this God has made Jesus Lord of all creation.

The grace of God is in all of us, but we still have problems in understanding this mystery—we have to try to penetrate it, though; the Resurrection is the basis of the mystery of the faith. The Shroud of Turin can be a help to our faith and devotion in this area.

Two Resurrection Miracles

And when Jesus had crossed again in the boat to the other side, a great crowd gathered about him; and he was beside the sea. Then came one of the rulers of the synagogue, Jairus by name; and seeing him, he fell at his feet, and besought him, saying,

"My little daughter is at the point of death. Come and lay your hands on her, so that she may be made well, and live." And he went with him. And a great crowd followed him and thronged about him. ... [and] there came from the ruler's house some who said, "Your daughter is dead. Why trouble the Teacher any further?" But ignoring what they said, Jesus said to the ruler of the synagogue, "Do not fear, only believe."

And he allowed no one to follow him except Peter and James and John the brother of James. When they came to the house of the ruler of the synagogue, he saw a tumult, and people weeping and wailing loudly. And when he had entered, he said to them, "Why do you make a tumult and weep? The child is not dead but sleeping." And they laughed at him. But he put them all outside, and took the child's father and mother and those who were with him, and went in where the child was. Taking her by the hand he said to her, "Talitha cumi"; which means, "Little girl, I say to you, arise." And immediately the girl got up and walked (she was twelve years of age), and they were immediately overcome with amazement. And he strictly charged them that no one should know this, and told them to give her something to eat. (Mark 5:21-24; 35-43).

The cry for help from the father of the child was a natural one: his daughter was dead by the time Jesus reached her, but Jesus told Jairus not to be afraid, but to have faith. Jesus showed His authority and told the girl to get up. So we shouldn't fear but believe. Our act of faith has to be continually renewed, so that it becomes a habit, one which allows us to live in God's presence. Each time we rise in the morning it's a sort of resurrection—when we turn away from God it's a sort of death, and we must appreciate this.

Thus, we must reflect on this teaching from God: Christ is rebuilding the work demolished by Adam. We will only be cured by faith—don't fear, only believe. Exterior acts of faith differ, but are the same in the depths of the heart, and become a turning to God; He stretches out His hand to us. Christians are called the "faithful"; those who cling to Christ. We always need to start again. Every moment we should believe; our act of faith is an act of abandonment. Jesus takes our hand too: He never stops doing this.

> Soon afterward he went to a city called Nain, and his disciples and a great crowd went with him. As he drew near to the gate of the city, behold, a man who had died was being carried out, the only son of his mother, and she was a widow; and a large crowd from the city was with her. And when the Lord saw her, he had compassion on her and said to her, "Do not weep." And he came and touched the bier, and the bearers stood still. And he said, "Young man, I say to you, arise." And the dead man sat up, and began to speak. And he gave him to his mother. Fear seized them all; and they glorified God, saying, "A great prophet has arisen among us!" and "God has visited his people!" And this report concerning him spread through the whole of Judea and all the surrounding country. (Luke 7:11-17).

When Jesus saw the widow He felt sorry for her; we need to understand this grace. Jesus' mind is a reflection of the mind of the Father, pitying us. The Heart of Jesus is full of mercy and compassion for us; it isn't just a question of feeling sorry for us. The pity of Jesus is His burning desire to come to our help in our deepest needs; we are like sheep without a shepherd. The Heart of Jesus is deeply moved by the solitude of Man.

The widow and her son represent humanity. We forget all this and go from one thing to another. Death is a consequence of sin: man wasn't supposed to die originally, since Adam had been given a special privilege of living without sin and death. But this privilege was lost by his sin and so sin is itself a sign of death. The pity of Jesus for this mother is a symbol of His pity for all humanity. He told the mother not to cry and gave her son back to her in a marvellous gesture expressive of His tenderness. In our own sadness, sorrow, and experience of death, including spiritual death through sin, the Lord comes and tells us rise up, like the widow's son. When we go to Confession we experience the tenderness of God who gives life back to His Church.

THE RESURRECTION & THE NEW CHRISTIAN LIFE

The Resurrection of Lazarus

Now a certain man was ill, Lazarus of Bethany, the village of Mary and her sister Martha. It was Mary who anointed the Lord with ointment and wiped his feet with her hair, whose brother Lazarus was ill. So the sisters sent to him, saying, "Lord, he whom you love is ill." But when Jesus heard it he said, "This illness is not unto death; it is for the glory of God, so that the Son of God may be glorified by means of it." Now Jesus loved Martha and her sister and Lazarus. So when he heard that he was ill, he stayed two days longer in the place where he was.

Then after this he said to the disciples, "Let us go into Judea again." The disciples said to him, "Rabbi, the Jews were but now seeking to stone you, and are you going there again?" Jesus answered, "Are there not twelve hours in the day? If any one walks in the day, he does not stumble, because he sees the light of this world. But if any one walks in the night, he stumbles, because the light is not in him."

Thus he spoke, and then he said to them, "Our friend Lazarus has fallen asleep, but I go to awake him out of sleep." The disciples said to him, "Lord, if he has fallen asleep, he will recover." Now Jesus had spoken of his death, but they thought that he meant taking rest in sleep. Then Jesus told them plainly, "Lazarus is dead; and for your sake I am glad that I was not there, so that you may believe. But let us go to him." Thomas, called the Twin, said to his fellow disciples, "Let us also go, that we may die with him." (John 11:1-16)

This miraculous resurrection has something more than similar miracles; Lazarus had been dead for some time, there is more insistence here. Jesus loved Lazarus and his sisters: He is our creator and redeemer and will raise us up too; He doesn't despair of us, even if we lack faith and give in to self-disgust. Jesus knew Lazarus wasn't damned, a victim of eternal death. The Father has never despaired of man; all the signs of tenderness we see in the world, as in the bond between parents and children, are signs which reflect the eternal concern in the Heart of Jesus for us.

Now when Jesus came, he found that Lazarus had already been in the tomb four days. Bethany was near Jerusalem, about two miles off, and many of the Jews had come to Martha and Mary to console them concerning their brother. When Martha heard that Jesus was coming, she went and met him, while Mary sat in the house. Martha said to Jesus, "Lord, if you had been here, my brother would not have died. And even now I know that whatever you ask from God, God will give you."

Jesus said to her, "Your brother will rise again." Martha said to him, "I know that he will rise again in the resurrection at the last day." Jesus said to her, "I am the resurrection and the life; he who believes in me, though he die, yet shall he live, and whoever lives and believes in me shall never die. Do you believe this?" She said to him, "Yes, Lord; I believe that you are the Christ, the Son of God, he who is coming into the world." (John 11:17-27)

There is a curious difference between the temperaments of Martha and Mary; one departs, the other remains in the house. Jesus said He was the resurrection and the life, those who believe in Him will never die; He then asked Martha if she believed this. These words of Jesus should be engraved on our hearts. We have this eternal life through grace. Don't be sentimental at funerals. Meditate on these very strong words of Jesus; they will work on our hearts if we allow them. It isn't just that Jesus has the power to resurrect—He is actually the resurrection and the life. Martha had boundless confidence in Jesus and believed He could raise her brother.

When she had said this, she went and called her sister Mary, saying quietly, "The Teacher is here and is calling for you." And when she heard it, she rose quickly and went to him. Now Jesus had not yet come to the village, but was still in the place where Martha had met him. When the Jews who were with her in the house, consoling her, saw Mary rise quickly and go out, they followed her, supposing that she was going to the tomb to weep there.

Then Mary, when she came where Jesus was and saw him, fell

at his feet, saying to him, "Lord, if you had been here, my brother would not have died." When Jesus saw her weeping, and the Jews who came with her also weeping, he was deeply moved in spirit and troubled; and he said, "Where have you laid him?" They said to him, "Lord, come and see." Jesus wept. So the Jews said, "See how he loved him!" But some of them said, "Could not he who opened the eyes of the blind man have kept this man from dying?" (John 11:28-37)

Martha called her sister Mary and she reacted in a very human way, saying to Jesus that her brother would not have died if He had been there.

Then Jesus, deeply moved again, came to the tomb; it was a cave, and a stone lay upon it. Jesus said, "Take away the stone." Martha, the sister of the dead man, said to him, "Lord, by this time there will be an odor, for he has been dead four days." Jesus said to her, "Did I not tell you that if you would believe you would see the glory of God?" So they took away the stone. And Jesus lifted up his eyes and said, "Father, I thank thee that thou hast heard me. I knew that thou hearest me always, but I have said this on account of the people standing by, that they may believe that thou didst send me." When he had said this, he cried with a loud voice, "Lazarus, come out."

The dead man came out, his hands and feet bound with bandages, and his face wrapped with a cloth. Jesus said to them, "Unbind him, and let him go." Many of the Jews therefore, who had come with Mary and had seen what he did, believed in him; but some of them went to the Pharisees and told them what Jesus had done. (John 11:38-46)

Jesus was deeply troubled by her tears and those of all the mourners. He told her not to fear but only believe. Then we come to a very important moment in the communication between the soul of Jesus and His Father. He spoke for the sake of all of us, so we would be able to believe in His mission.

We can stress three things which these resurrection accounts tell us. Firstly, we should see the disappearance of eternal life in us caused by loss of faith as something which is worse than physical death. This faith is a barometer of our interior understanding and can be diminished by despair and fear. So we need to make a big effort to preserve our faith. Secondly, we need to hear from others of the tenderness of God. This is particularly the role of Priests. They shouldn't be like Moses giving laws; they must preach Christ so that He is written on our hearts, not with ink but with the grace of the Holy Spirit. Thirdly, the resurrection is a reality which is still to be fully lived and experienced by us. We constantly need to be awoken to hear "Don't fear, only believe": we need to hear this from others, so for the great majority of people complete solitude is not a good idea—we're not capable of living in this way really.

The Meaning of the Resurrection

Faith has to be expressed. We can make acts of faith during the day. We Christians rarely have enough compassion; we are in danger of becoming like rich, indolent people. True compassion involves faith too; we need to pray for this. The Holy Spirit should arouse us to another sort of pity. The Church is for the humble and the poor; not for the rich who want to dominate through a dead faith. The person who has lost faith is without eternal life; such a person is really the poorest of the poor.

These three Gospel accounts of resurrections all anticipated Christ's Resurrection and look forward to our own. The Resurrection of Jesus was of another order, not in a purely spatial or temporal dimension. His resurrected body was a true body, the same one conceived by Mary, but with a new spiritual dimension. Those who live for the Spirit are full of life. The risen Christ will never die; He gives life and has risen in the flesh in a true body, but isn't confined like us any more. Christ is in the depths of our souls, with us when we pray. We should become more aware of this, and try to experience and understand it; this is very important for us. The Eucharistic presence of Jesus through transubstantiation is linked to our belief in the resurrection. The risen body is present in the Eucharist, the body marked with the wounds of the Crucifixion, and we shouldn't be incredulous like Thomas.

Jesus wanted through His tenderness to give us a sign, and so this power of consecration is given to priests. Bread becomes the infinite, extraordinary, intensive presence of God, the presence of the risen Christ, body, blood, soul, and divinity. There is a great mystery of faith here. The risen Christ is truly the head of the Church, and there is no true Church, no true unity without this Resurrection. All this would have been impossible if Christ hadn't risen; He never stops giving us life. We must meditate on these texts and realise them in our life. The resurrection from the dead is the visible sign of the power of God and the source of the Church's vitality. Unlike the three people in the Gospel accounts who were raised bodily to die again, our final resurrection will be to a new birth and immortality.

The birth of her child is painful for a woman but leads to joy. If we are raised then we are baptised as new creatures, new sons and adopted brothers of Jesus. We don't stop being reborn, resurrected—it is a dynamic process, continual. Where sin abounds, mercy and grace are more abundant. The source of the resurrection is the Father. We are always dying and being raised to life. Resurrection is a sign of divine power, proof of God's supremacy. The Father raised Jesus; this is emphasised in the Acts of the Apostles. We must imitate Jesus, and also allow ourselves to be "raised." It is important to realise that Jesus' will to obey His Father led to His Resurrection. His Baptism signified His complete obedience.

So the risen Christ participates in all the activities of the Trinity. The Word of God with the Father breathes the Holy Spirit; this is the stupendous love of God for us. Our prayers should be at this level, at the level of the sublime. The resurrected Christ can't die—He gives life. We should meditate on the fact that the resurrected Christ isn't in space-time: He has a transcendent body which is spiritual. He is present everywhere, but especially in our hearts when we are in a state of grace.

> He is the image of the invisible God, the first-born of all creation; for in him all things were created, in heaven and on earth, visible and invisible, whether thrones or dominions or principalities or authorities—all things were created through him and for him. He is before all things, and in him all things hold together. He is the head of the body, the church; he is the beginning, the first-born from the dead, that in everything he might be preeminent. For in him all the fulness of God was pleased to dwell, and through him to reconcile to himself all things, whether on earth or in heaven, making peace by the blood of his cross. (Col 1:15-20)

The apostles didn't recognize Jesus on the road to Emmaus; it was only when they reached the inn that their eyes were opened. We discover the Christ of the Resurrection through Faith. We need to recognize Him and this can only really take place in our hearts, just as the disciple's hearts burned within them.

> So they drew near to the village to which they were going. He appeared to be going further, but they constrained him, saying, "Stay with us, for it is toward evening and the day is now far spent." So he went in to stay with them. When he was at table with them, he took the bread and blessed, and broke it, and gave it to them. And their eyes were opened and they recognized him; and he vanished out of their sight. They said to each other, "Did not our hearts burn within us while he talked to us on the road, while he opened to us the Scriptures?" (Luke 24:28-32)

The risen Christ is the dynamic principle of life. This should be, for us, a missionary life. The action of Jesus continues in the Mass as a present realization—it is the permanent today of God. The presence of God as the Lord is only perceived by faith as an interior thing. We are sensitive to this in proportion to our interior life. Marthe said, "Our life is proportional to the quality of our contemplation." It is very important for us to fully realize this ourselves. The eyes of the disciples were finally opened; we need to aim for this. We need to pray that the grace of the priesthood, as intermediaries, will lead to the laity becoming better Christians. We should go to God through the Priest—this is the best way. God makes the Church with fallible human beings, but all of us have a responsibility for mission. Jesus gives us His peace, but not as the world gives it. Peace comes from the risen Lord.

18

The Gift of Self & the
Consecration to Jesus through Mary

The Church is born primarily of Christ's total self-giving for our
salvation, anticipated in the institution of the Eucharist and
fulfilled on the cross. (CCC 766)

We should give ourselves fully to God, a gift of the whole self,
given with humble obedience and courage. Obedience should
be the axis of our life. God asks us to give ourselves up to His
love. St Thérèse spoke of how God protected her; she became
his chosen bride at the Carmel at Lisieux. The world needs
holy, fruitful lives, like that of St Thérèse. This involves a
total gift of self and the language of bride and groom. It
demands from all of us a renunciation of our own powers,
faculties, wishes, expectations and personal hopes. It is a form
of death which may displease us at first but which will get us
to the heart of things and cause us to marvel at the goodness
of God.

God wants everything—a total gift of self. This gift of self
is the best nourishment we can give people today: a real
person and not just dead works. By our actions we show that
this new life is actually here, a reality. Love transforms life
into beauty. We should look after our bodies but not to the
exclusion of spiritual matters: nothing is achieved without
prayer and communion. We must make a full gift of self—this

is a simple thing but demands humility and a recognition of our weakness and our need to lean on God. When we become small we will be raised up by God. This offering of self gives reality to life. The way we do our job is more important than what the job actually is. Man is sacred because he offers himself to God. Our fruitfulness is proportional to our holiness.

The life of a human being goes towards God. We come from God and we return to Him. We should seek to give ourselves to others and to God. Jesus was offered to God by His parents, in the Temple. Most religions demand some sort of offering—we should offer of our best, the first fruits of our lives.

The Gift of Self

Jesus was offered to His Father through the hands of Joseph and Mary. The world was renewed by the offering of the wills of Jesus and Mary. We need to make an offering of our freedom, will and intelligence, even though this isn't very fashionable. If we don't give ourselves to God, and others, then we will suffer from a sort of "spiritual cancer." We should offer ourselves with Jesus—this was Marthe's approach; to offer ourselves to God with Jesus, as in the Third Eucharistic Prayer. St Louis de Montfort is an example of someone who made a total offering of self to God.

Marthe said we should offer our body with all its senses, our soul with all its thoughts, our will, our heart with all its affections; our works, sufferings, struggles—everything—all offered to God in Jesus with Mary and the Priest. Through Him, with Him and in Him, we make a total offering with joy. We have received freely so we should give freely and with joy. We must offer the best of our faculties to God and not be like Cain. Simple gestures count; we shouldn't give God or other people the poor rubbish of our lives, that which is left over. We need to become living offerings.

The early Church held everything in common; so for us everything should be given; it doesn't matter how small our offering is, what is important is not to keep anything back for ourselves. We shouldn't be like Ananias and Sapphira who tried to deceive the Holy Spirit. Our offering must be from the heart and not just a question of rules or duty. Give all to God.

We should pray and offer sacrifices so that all our friends and relatives may be saved, so that we really show our love for them. We must offer and pray for those who are dear to us. Marthe prayed unceasingly for all the inhabitants of her local area: she offered herself totally. But she was also tempted to give up by the devil—"Haven't you done enough already?"

Our soul shouldn't be turned in on itself, but opened up for all. The world needs generous souls like Marthe, people prepared to offer their sufferings to God through Jesus. We must look at all aspects of our life: our spirit, will, heart, intentions, actions, thoughts, desires—look for everything which is too human, too natural, everything which is not perfectly Christian. We must tear out the bad things every day, become more "divine" every day. In particular, Marthe said that resentment is something we have to eliminate at all costs. Our offering must be pure like that of the Priest. We must renew our offering continually: every day we should show Jesus to other people. We can't be dynamic without giving our lives fully to God.

Consecration to Jesus through Mary

We need to renew our consecration to Jesus through Mary every day; we are always tending to fall away from this. An important part of a Foyer retreat is the "Consecration to Jesus through Mary." Marthe was introduced to the writings of St Louis de Montfort, particularly his *True Devotion*, and she recognized his spirit was for her. St Louis wanted to give Mary her proper place in a civilization which was losing its bearings. The fact that the style of this "Consecration" is of the eighteenth century shouldn't put us off; we should enjoy the style. There isn't a particular need to update it, as sometimes this can change the thought of the author. The consecration to Mary emphasizes her position at the heart of the Church. Mary is important, the Mother of God who was conceived without sin. Paul VI pronounced her "Mother of the Church." The Consecration means giving ourselves entirely to Christ and turning away from evil. These two aspects are important. St Louis's description of Christ as the Incarnate Wisdom implies that He is the perfect embodiment of right thinking, which when speaking of God reaches its highest form in the second person of the Trinity. Our aim should be to carry our cross after Jesus and follow Him. We all start from the position of being unfaithful sinners who need to try and be better than before.

We need to renew our commitment to God continually—we tend to forget. We need to learn from our experiences. This isn't a fatalistic attitude; we do the best we can and leave the impossible to God. We can't have too strict a plan for life but must be open to the Spirit. There needs to be a great delicacy in dealing with the Holy Spirit—we can't lay down rigid laws. We must leave God with full permission to dispose of us as He wants, and particularly we must be open to His will. Our "submission" should involve chains of love, as lived by Marthe, and not a strict slavery. But we can be slaves to events at times.

The "slavery of love" for Mary is something wonderful. She has been favored with power over the whole Church. She was born without sin for us. She is immaculate for us and because of us. The Church speaks of the blessed fault of Adam which has brought us such a Redeemer. We must discover the meaning of all this in everyday life. Goodness, gentleness, and patience make people see sense; Mary is the Queen of all these virtues. She brings people back. Goodness and gentleness change people. The Magnificat shows that Mary was aware of her greatness but also dependent on God; there is no false modesty there. Marthe never gave a full description of Mary—she is too beautiful for words; and likewise, St Bernadette also couldn't possibly compare her to any statue she had seen.

Prayer to Christ Jesus

Christ Jesus, eternal and Incarnate Wisdom, true God and true man, only son of the Father and of Mary ever virgin, I adore you in the unity of your divine life with the Father for all eternity and in the virgin womb of your Mother Mary at the time of your incarnation. I thank you for having "emptied yourself to assume the condition of a slave even to accepting death on a cross," in order to free us from the power of the devil. I praise you and glorify you for having been willing to submit to Mary, your most holy Mother, in all things, in order to put us, through her, in a state of free belonging and of total love towards you. Thanks to her, I hope to obtain from you contrition and the forgiveness of my sins and my growth in divine love.

Salute to Mary

I salute you, then, Mary Immaculate, living tabernacle of the Holy Trinity, beloved daughter of the Father, mother of the incarnate Word, completely associated with his work of incarnation and of redemption, Spouse of the Holy Spirit in the animation of the Church. I salute you, queen of heaven and earth, whose power extends over all the orders of creation. I salute you, sure refuge of sinners whose merciful heart is open to every suffering of the body and the soul. Inspire in me a burning desire of sanctity and lead me towards perfect charity by the light and force of your love.

Consecration to the Blessed Virgin Mary

Wishing to die to sin, in order to live for God in Jesus Christ, I renew and ratify today, in your hands, Mary, the vows of my Baptism, I forever renounce Satan, his spirit and his works, and I give myself entirely to Jesus Christ, my Saviour and my God, to live with him as an adopted child of the Father and to work for his Kingdom. I accept to bear my cross and follow him, all the days of my life, in order to collaborate in the redemption, and I wish to be completely faithful to Him.

I choose you today, Mary, in the presence of the saints and angels of heaven, for my mother and my queen. I deliver and consecrate to you, in full submission and love, my body and my soul, my freedom, my intelligence and my will, all my faculties and all my worldly goods. I give up to you even the value of my good actions, past, present and future, leaving you the entire right to dispose of me and of all that belongs to me, without exception, however you wish, for the greater glory of God in time and in eternity.

Beloved Mother, receive the gift of my freedom, in union with Christ who was submissive to you in your divine maternity, in homage to the power which he has given you over the Holy Church, in thanksgiving for the "great things" which the Blessed Trinity has accomplished in you. Fully recognizing the maternity which Jesus gave you over me while dying on the cross, I affirm that from now on I want to remain in total filiation towards you, to seek your honor, and to obey you in all things.

Admirable Mother present me to your beloved Son, that I may be forever bound to him by a bond of unchanging love, so that, having redeemed me through you, he may also receive me through you. Mother of mercy, give me the grace to obtain full possession of him who is the wisdom and joy of the Father, and to count me, for that, among the number of those whom you love, teach, lead, nourish, and protect as your children.

Faithful Virgin Mary, make of me in all things a disciple full of love and an apostle full of faith in Jesus Christ your Son, so that, by your example and your intercession, I may arrive at the fullness of his age on earth and of his glory in heaven. Amen.

Further Reading

In English

Fr Raymond Peyret, *Marthe Robin: The Cross and the Joy*, (Alba House, New York, 1983).

Fr Michel Tierny, Martin Blake & David Fanning, *Marthe Robin: A Chosen Soul*, (Catholic Truth Society, London, 1999), B652, CTS Booklets.

Both of these books are obtainable via the Theotokos site at: www./theotokos.org.uk/pages/pages/onlinebs/onlinebs.html

Fr Raymond Peyret's book, *Marthe Robin: The Cross and the Joy* is available in the United States from Amazon.com via: www.amazon.com/exec/obidos/ASIN/081890464X/theotokos cath-20

In French

Fr Raymond Peyret, *Prends ma Vie, Seigneur: La Longe Masse de Marthe Robin*, (Desclee de Brouwer, 1985).

Fr Bernard Peyrous, *Vie de Marthe Robin,* (Emmanuel, 2006), 362 pages, 20 euros, ISBN: 2915313636

Many other books in French on Marthe Robin are also available. These can be obtained from: www.amazon.fr

For Further information contact:

English Friends of the Foyers, 4 Dunkerton Close, Glastonbury, BA6 8LZ England. email: mblake@onetel.net.uk

www.theotokos.org.uk/pages/movecomm/foyer/foyer.html

Contact the Irish Friends at: edwardjdonaghy@eircom.net

In recent years Foyer retreats in English have taken place during the summer at the Foyer at Tressaint in Brittany, France. This will continue in 2007, and hopefully beyond. Retreats last five days, in silence, with three talks each day. Retreatants join the community for morning and evening prayer, the Mass, and Rosary each day. Donations of approximately 36 Euros, (£25), per day would be appreciated.

Tressaint can be reached by air from Britain via Dinard on Ryanair, or by sea from Portsmouth to St Malo, or from Plymouth to Roscoff. The Foyer at Tressaint is about 15 miles from St Malo.

If you would like further information please e-mail Fr David Hartley at: Dm.Hartley@tesco.net

or the Tressaint Foyer at: foyer.tressaint@wanadoo.fr

The Tressaint web site can be seen at: www.tressaint.com

Foyer de Charité de Tressaint, B.P. 145, 22104 Dinan Cedex, France. Tel: 02 96 85 86 00.

For further information on the Foyers of Charity worldwide and on Marthe Robin, see: www.foyer-de-charite.com/

In the United States see: www.foyerofcharity.com

By the same author

Understanding Medjugorje: Heavenly Visions or Religious Illusion? (Theotokos, Nottingham, 2006)

Foreword by Father Peter Joseph
Preface by Prof Arpad Szackolczai

ISBN 0955074606 - 310pp - £14.95

This book is an in-depth investigation into some of the most surprising, but also most influential, spiritual phenomena to have affected modern Catholicism. Millions of people have visited the site of the alleged visions of the Blessed Virgin Mary in Bosnia-Herzegovina, despite the fact that they have received no official Church approval.

In reading *Understanding Medjugorje* you will discover:

How important Church figures, including Pope John Paul II and Cardinal Ratzinger—now Benedict XVI—have actually viewed Medjugorje, as well as the role of influential priests and theologians in its promotion. The links between the visions, the Charismatic Renewal, and the worldwide Medjugorje movement are also explored. In addition, the book analyzes how Medjugorje compares with Fatima, and what the successive local bishops of Mostar have said about it.

"Understanding Medjugorje *raises important questions about Medjugorje, questions which no sensible Catholic can ignore.*"
— Fr Peter Joseph STD, Chancellor of the Maronite Diocese of Australia

"*Donal Foley's work, and this book in particular, by connecting religious experiences and practices to crucial questions about the emergence of contemporaryculture, is a major step forward in this field.*"
— Prof Arpad Szakolczai, Sociology Department, University College Cork

To order please visit:
www.theotokos.org.uk/pages/books/mariapps/mariapps.html

or you can order via online booksellers or through your local bookseller.

By the same author

Marian Apparitions, the Bible, and the Modern World

Foreword by Fr Aidan Nichols OP

Imprimatur from Bishop McMahon of Nottingham, England

ISBN 0852443137 - 374pp - £19.99

This is an in depth investigation into the major Marian apparitions that have occurred during the last five centuries. It relates them to secular happenings and important revolutionary events in Western history including the Reformation and the French and Russian Revolutions. It also argues that the major apparitions are not random or historically inconsequential events, but actually seem to follow a preordained plan, one intimately linked with the biblical Marian typology explored by the Church Fathers. In particular, this books looks at the importance of Fatima in the life of the Church, its links with the papacy, and its continuing relevance for the Third Millennium.

"With his Marian Apparitions, the Bible, and the Modern World, Donal Foley has made a very important contribution to our understanding and appreciation of private revelations, in particular those of Our Lady. ... Not only ... scholars and believers, but the general public will find this volume informative and inspirational."
                                                                    - Fr. Peter M. Fehlner, F.I.

"Donal Foley has written a book with an extraordinary message."
                                                                    - Fr Aidan Nichols OP

To order please visit:
www.theotokos.org.uk/pages/books/mariapps/mariapps.html

or: www.amazon.co.uk/exec/obidos/ASIN/0852443137/theotokoscath-21

or you can order via online booksellers or through your local bookseller.

Lightning Source UK Ltd.
Milton Keynes UK
17 April 2010

152981UK00001B/5/A